SYNTHETIC DYES

FOR NATURAL FIBERS

Synthetic
Dyes for
Natural
Fibers

Much luck in creating your rainbows!

LINDA KNUTSON

Linda Knutson

Madrona Publishers   **Seattle**   **1982**

Revised edition, 1986
First Printing: 5M:686:OB
Second Printing: 3M:188:OB

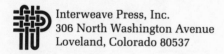 Interweave Press, Inc.
306 North Washington Avenue
Loveland, Colorado 80537

Library of Congress Catalog #86-080912
ISBN #0-934026-23-8

Acknowledgments

My deepest appreciation to those who provided help and encouragement during the writing of this book, especially Lynn Daly who offered invaluable assistance in so many areas and her husband Brian, who provided some of the photographs. And a warm thanks to Rosie Winters who generously assisted with the photography for the second edition.

I would also like to give special thanks to Virginia Harvey and Jean Wilson for taking the time to read the manuscript and encouraging me to seek publication.

To all of those who helped with the many aspects of putting a book together—modeling garments, providing props for photos, offering suggestions for the manuscript, tracking down reference material and much, much more—my most appreciative thanks.

Technical assistance was generously given by Ron Granich of Cerulean Blue Ltd., Seattle, whose *Dye Chemistry Notebook* and acid dye instructions were valuable references for preparing certain sections of the book.

Although they prefer to remain anonymous I also want to express my gratitude for the invaluable help I received from several dye industry people. They never tired of answering my questions and were most generous in providing me with technical material.

The artists whose work is illustrated represent a cross-section of fiber artists in the country. I appreciate their loaning me their slides so that others can be inspired by their work. (Their names are listed with their work.)

And, finally, thank you to my husband Ron for his invaluable technical assistance and especially his encouragement in preparing the revised portion of the manuscript for the second edition.

In memory of Dave

Contents

Introduction

I have always had an innate curiosity about the world around me. I was one of those children always asking *why* — which explains my decision to major in the sciences in college. And it explains why, four years later with a diploma in hand, I went to work doing research in a laboratory. This was my life for five years, after which my husband and I moved to a small farm in central Washington where research facilities did not exist. So I set up my own facilities; I turned my attentions to nature's laboratory and began exploring and experimenting with natural dyes. My stove became my Bunsen burner and my dyepots were my test tubes.

For the next couple of years I spent many long, wonderful hours with pruning shears in one hand and a sack in the other, collecting just about anything that grew. Even my garden did not escape my ever-present pruning shears, and eventually I set aside a growing area as my "dye patch." Along with corn, tomatoes and beans I hoed coreopsis, marigolds and weld.

With each new batch of plant material that found its way to my laboratory, I experienced much excitement as I impatiently waited for the moment when the yarn was finally ready to be removed from the dyepot and reveal the hidden colors of my latest find. Gradually, I accumulated a large stock of yarn samples of beautiful muted colors in shades of orange, green, yellow and brown. However, except for what I got from some of the lichens, I was rarely able to produce brighter colors from the plant material found locally. Only by purchasing such exotic-sounding things as cochineal, brazilwood, logwood and madder could I obtain certain colors; but these purchased materials were expensive and, more important, I had no personal involvement in collecting them. So I figured that if I was going to have to buy the dye material in order to obtain a wider range of colors, why not try the synthetic dyes?

Also, at about the same time, I found that I was becoming increasingly fascinated with color and the use of color in weaving. Again, the natural dyes were not able to provide me with the palette I now wanted. About six months previously I had had a brief introduction to the Kiton dyes during a color workshop but, since the dyeing portion of the workshop was only for demonstrating color movement (the progression from one color to another) and not for working with the dyes, I essentially had to start from scratch. My appetite had been whetted, though, by seeing the many beautiful, bright and, yes, subtle colors that were possible.

When I originally began working with the natural dyes, I found many books and articles to serve as guides but, when it came to synthetic dyes, investigation revealed that very little written material was available other than the basic information furnished by distributors. So it was back to the laboratory—my kitchen—to begin brewing up some color with the synthetic dyes. First, I mixed yellow with blue in equal proportions, expecting to get the green on my color wheel. Instead, a blue-green was produced. I tried the same thing by combining 50:50 amounts of yellow and red and this time got a red-orange, not orange as expected. The synthetic dyes did not behave like their theoretical counterparts on the color wheel. This meant that I would have to create my own dye recipes for a color wheel through a process of systematic color mixing to determine the formulas. From this point, I decided, I would further expand my experimenting to include all the shades that could be produced—again following a systematic approach—from just the five primaries: red, yellow, blue, turquoise and magenta. The range of colors that could be obtained was incredible and, by keeping accurate records and being precise with my measurements, I was able to reproduce all of these colors. The implications of this were exciting. My yarn inventory could be reduced to just the basic whites, naturals and grays in various textures since now, in my laboratory, I could dye the yarns any color I chose. An unlimited color palette was possible.

My scientific background allowed me to work with the dyes using the equipment and techniques of the scientist. This was important because it enabled me to accurately measure the dyes, which is absolutely essential for color reproducibility. Unfortunately, unfamiliarity with these techniques and equipment was preventing many fiber people from employing these methods. This is one of my reasons for writing this book. Once the theories, processes and techniques involved are laid out in a clear and straightforward manner, anyone who desires to can master the dyer's art. A key part of the technique is use of the stock solution method, which means that the dyes are measured as liquids instead of powders. An expensive scale is needed to measure dyes accurately in the powder form while inexpensive, easy-to-use equipment is available for measuring liquids.

Before the dyer's art can be mastered, however, an understanding of color is also necessary; color, after all, is the business of the dyer. For this reason I have presented color theory, with emphasis on how it applies to the work of the dyer, discussed color mixing systems and offered suggestions for systematically developing an inventory of color formulas. Such an inventory will aid dyers in obtaining their own stock of color recipes and samples (called "patterns" by the dye industry), and will eliminate much of the time-consuming experimentation that a dyer would otherwise have to do. Because of the numerous color combinations that exist, it is unlikely that any one person could ever try them all, but a systematic approach brings a sense of order to the process.

Equally important to mastering the dyer's art is a knowledge of the various synthetic dyes, since they provide the means of producing the colors. While many dyes are available to the home dyer, some are easier to work with than others because they possess certain desirable properties including good mixing ability; production of bright colors (which allows for mixing both intense hues and subtle shades); fastness (the colors do not fade appreciably when exposed to sunlight and washing); and ease and safety in use. These are the "workhorse" dyes, and they include the leveling acid dyes for the protein fibers (which include wool) and the fiber-reactive dyes for cellulose (which includes cotton). With just these two types of synthetic dyes, the person working with natural fibers can meet most color needs.

So that the dyer can choose the best type of dye for a project and understand and, therefore, control what is happening in the dyepot, I have discussed the chemical and physical nature of the workhorse dyes. I have included information on the chemistry of the dye-fiber reaction, the purpose of the various chemicals used in dyeing, the individual properties of the dyes and how they affect the results. In addition, specific dye instructions for the fiber-reactive and leveling acid dyes are included. While each process is specific to the dye, the basic method for calculating the ingredients (water, dyes, chemicals) is the same. This means that the dyer can become familiar and comfortable with the procedure in just a short time.

I have also presented an overview of the properties and chemical nature of the other synthetic dyes suitable for use with natural fibers. While specific dyeing instructions are not included for these dyes (instructions are available from the distributors), most of the techniques, theory and general procedures given here can be applied to them. With the information in this book, the fiber person should be able to master the dyer's art and work confidently with any dyes.

SYNTHETIC DYES
FOR NATURAL FIBERS

1. Why Become A Dyer?

Whether to become a dyer is a decision every fiber person, including the weaver, knitter, crocheter and even the seamstress, en-
counters at some point in his or her work. Perhaps it is because a
particular shade of yarn or fabric cannot be found. Or, quite
possibly, the question has arisen because of the limited color
range of the marvelous textured yarns being offered today. While
the commercial yarn companies produce an amazing variety of
yarns in what at first glance appears to be every imaginable color,
it becomes apparent on closer examination that many colors are
not available, especially the tints and tones. After spending hours,
or possibly days, searching for a particular shade of yarn with no
luck, the fiber person is likely to start thinking, "If only I could dye
some yarn that color."

So why isn't everyone who works with fiber also a dyer? Probably the most important reasons are the person's lack of aware-
ness of the versatility of the synthetic dyes and the simplicity of
working with them, and the absence of instructions geared to the
fiber person who doesn't have a scientific background. Both of
these points will be dealt with in detail later in the book. For now,
it is important for prospective dyers to further explore the many
benefits, both practical and artistic, that result from the ability to
dye and will encourage the fiber person to take advantage of the
many opportunities available to the dyer.

Practical Benefits of Dyeing

Probably the most important of the practical benefits of dyeing
are economic. A fiber person is no different from anyone else in
being concerned about the ever-increasing cost of supplies,

3

which in this case usually translates into yarns.

By examining the buying habits of a "typical" fiber person it is possible to discover areas where yarn costs can be cut. One common practice of this typical person is to invest in a large inventory of commercially dyed yarn to be used at some future date for as yet unidentified projects. Some of the yarns represent impulse buys—perhaps exciting novelty yarns—while others may reflect the colors the person feels comfortable using.

Regardless of why the colors have been chosen, it is not until a project has been designed that the actual color choices are made and the needed amounts of yarn are calculated. At this time of reckoning the fiber person may discover that an insufficient

For the dyer who uses synthetic dyes, the yarn inventory can be reduced to a general stock of white, off-white, natural, and gray yarns in various textures and fibers.

amount of a particular yarn is on hand or that other colors than those available would be preferable. This means additional money and time will be spent purchasing the necessary yarns, while the capital previously invested in the yarn inventory remains tied up. This does not make sound economic sense.

The typical fiber person, when buying commercial yarns for a specific project, also must often purchase an additional skein of each color to be certain of sufficient quantities. This is necessary because variations in color occur between different commercial dyeings. If extra skeins have not been opened they can sometimes be returned, but even if only a small amount has been used, the fiber person is simply stuck with the rest of the skein. A large inventory of odd quantities remaining from various projects builds up over the years, eventually representing a substantial capital investment. It is not unusual for these yarns to sit on a shelf or in a drawer for years before a project can be designed for them.

Dyers, instead, can invest the money budgeted for yarns in a general stock of whites, naturals, beiges and grays in a variety of textures, to be dyed as needed. Since color decisions are not involved, such yarns can be purchased in quantity, often at a discount. White and pale shades of mill ends also can be bought quite reasonably.

When a specific project is contemplated, the initial planning step commonly involves making samples to determine yarn and color choices. Then, small amounts (as little as one-third of an ounce) of the basic yarn stock can be accurately dyed whatever colors are to be tried. When the final yarn and color decisions are made, the amounts of yarns needed can be calculated and larger quantities dyed to match the samples chosen. If it turns out that an insufficient amount was dyed it is simply a matter, later on, of throwing some more fiber into the dyepot. With careful record-keeping and good laboratory techniques, the home dyer can exactly match previously dyed colors.

So the dyer not only has the opportunity to save money when purchasing yarns but also does not need to keep money tied up indefinitely in an unnecessarily large inventory. Equally important, the dyer is able to color only the quantity of yarns required for a project. This becomes especially important when working with the expensive textured yarns, where any amount wasted is costly.

In addition to these economic advantages, the dyer realizes the convenience of being able to create any color while using the

basic yarn stock. The actual dyeing procedure is simple to perform and requires just over an hour's time to complete. The bulk
of the time is spent "cooking" the yarn, so the dyer can read a
book or perhaps warp a loom at the same time.

Compare the above situation to that of the fiber person who
depends on predyed yarns. While some fiber people are fortunate

Two mill-end yarns and a bouclé yarn were dyed to match the color of the leather used for
the yoke of this jacket. The unified color allows the texture contrasts to be emphasized.

enough to have one or more well-supplied yarn shops in their
area, many are not so lucky and often must purchase their yarns
from mail-order sources. This not only results in a delay in
starting a project but also creates problems caused by making
color decisions based on only the small snip of fiber displayed in

the yarn brochure.

Colors are like the chameleon, changing shades depending on the surroundings. Because of this effect that one color has on another, it is not uncommon for the fiber artist to make color

A commercial white wool sweater purchased on sale was dyed a shade of teal blue to coordinate with a particular outfit.

changes when all the skeins are seen together. This means it's back to studying the yarn brochures and ordering additional yarns. The dyer, however, needs only to throw some yarn into the dyepot to acquire the needed colors. The time spent dyeing is more than compensated for by saving many hours of searching the yarn shops for a particular shade or the delay of waiting for the mailman.

Artistic Benefits of Dyeing

In addition to the practical advantages of dyeing, there are artistic benefits as well. No longer must color decisions be based on what is commercially available. For the dyer, an unlimited palette is possible, providing great control over colors. This means projects can be designed using color in many subtle

For this patterned raanu vest, the basic weft yarn was formed into twenty-two small skeins that were then dyed in a harmonious range of shades. See close-up in color section.

shade and tone variations that would not be possible with commercial yarns. Almost anything is possible. If, for example, the colors of nature are to be matched—such as the blue petal of a delphinium or the autumn tone of a leaf—the dyer is able to mix colors that exactly copy Mother Nature's.

Equally important is the personal involvement with each shade pulled from the dyepot. The ability to create color can be inspirational; thoughts and ideas are born that lead to further

Jupitarian Light (43 inches by 38 inches), by Ruth E. Anderson. The subtle color movement of this piece could only be achieved by custom dyeing. Photo courtesy of the artist.

experiments in color mixing, with many unusual and beautiful results. Only by dyeing is it possible to create the more subtle color effects and moods. Because there are no limits to the colors available, color movement can be explored to any degree. Imagination is the only limiting factor. Even with the large number of colors offered by some of the Swedish yarn companies there are too many gaps to make a workable palette.

Properties of the Ideal Dye

In order to realize all of the advantages of being a dyer, the fiber artist has to consider the properties which are necessary in a dye to fulfill the previously discussed benefits. Table 1 lists these properties. Any dye which meets these criteria will be able to satisfy most needs of the home dyer.

Of the many dyes currently available, two main types fulfill the requirements in the following table. These are the leveling acid dyes for the protein fibers, such as wool, and the fiber-reactive

TABLE 1

PROPERTIES OF THE IDEAL DYE

PROPERTY	IMPORTANCE
Brightness of Colors	Allows for the mixing of both intense colors and subtle shades.
Good Mixing Ability	Eliminates the need to stock a large number of dyes. The majority of colors can be mixed using just the primary hues.
Color Reproducibility	Allows colors to be duplicated. Depends on good mixing ability to produce consistent dyeing results.
Even Dyeing Ability	Assures streak-free dyeing.
Economy	Allows for low-cost dyeing.
Fastness	Assures little color change from fading caused by sunlight or normal conditions of washing.
Ease of Use	Requires only a simple dyeing procedure.
Safety	Assures that the dyes do not contain toxic chemicals and the dyeing procedure does not use harmful ingredients.
Substantivity	Refers to the affinity of the dye for the fiber; important in a dye to be used for exhaust (waterbath) dyeing, which is the method used by the home dyer for dyeing yarns and fabric.
Full Primary Color Range	Allows for the mixing of most other colors using just a basic inventory of primary dyes.

dyes for the cellulose fibers, such as cotton. Because these dyes offer so many advantages, they are the most widely used by the synthetic dyer and will be considered in much greater detail in the following chapters.

On occasion, specific requirements in a project will require the use of other types of dyes. Although these other dyes do not meet all of the criteria of the "ideal dye," their unique properties may allow them to meet the special demands of a project. Superior washfastness, for example, is the main consideration when selecting a type of dye to use for a felting project, which must endure severe washing conditions when it is produced. Unfortunately, the dyes noted for superior washfastness do not produce bright colors. But bright colors are of little importance if the dyes are going to fade when washed. When choosing a dye, it is important to consider the needs of the project as well as the properties of the dye.

The Synthetic Dye Myth

Although many people who work with fibers are familiar with the natural dyes, they often resist working with the synthetic dyes. Their lack of enthusiasm is reflected in the absence of literature on the subject. Many books and pamphlets are available to the person using natural dyes, but the person using synthetic dyes has apparently been overlooked. Perhaps this is because of the prejudice many people seem to have for these dyes—feeling, unjustly, that it is only with the natural dyes that the beautiful, subtle shades can be achieved. Misuse of synthetic dyes and lack of color mixing knowledge are largely responsible for this bias. But, with proper understanding and handling, the dyer can create any color desired with synthetic dyes. Every shade and tone produced with the natural dyes can be duplicated with the synthetic dyes—and the process is easier and less time-consuming.

Linda Ligon, in her article in *interweave*, Vol.III no.3 (Spring, 1978), offers the following explanation for the lack of literature on the synthetic dyes. Chemical dyeing, she points out, first came into being in the mid-nineteenth century—about the same time home textile production was disappearing. With the revival of weaving and other crafts in recent times, there was a corresponding rejection of any methods that hinted of modern technology. Instead, in a fit of nostalgia, craft people went back to the methods used by their great-grandparents, which included natural dyeing. Even today many fiber people feel strongly that they should do everything the "natural way," a rationalization based purely on emotion. Emotions are, of course, very much involved in every fiber piece created—but the artist needs a more open-minded approach to take advantage of new developments and techniques. There is a proper place for every method.

2. Fiber and Dye Chemistry

History of the Synthetic Dyes

Prior to the discovery of the synthetic dyes, all dyes came from natural materials, which were largely of plant and animal origin. Although many plants will yield a dye that can be used to color fiber, only a few, throughout all of history, have been known to produce bright shades. And quite often those dyes that gave the most beautiful bright colors were difficult to acquire or required a laborious extraction process. The beautiful red dye cochineal, for example, requires approximately 70,000 insects to produce a pound of the dye. These insects, *Dactylopius coccus*, are found only on certain cacti in Mexico and must be hand picked, making the collection process time-consuming and expensive. Another well-known example is the dye royal purple, which comes from a shellfish on the eastern Mediterranean coast; 8,500 animals were needed to produce one gram of dye, making purple material so costly that only the rich could afford it.

It was because of these expensive dyes and laborious collection procedures that the synthetic dye industry came into being. The British were especially interested in developing inexpensive synthetic dyes and offered money as a prize to anyone who could develop such materials. As often happens, however, the first synthetic dye was discovered by accident—by W.H. Perkin, in 1856. While trying to produce quinine synthetically from coal tar, Perkin stumbled onto a compound that instead produced the color mauve when dissolved in alcohol. Since this compound was derived from aniline, a coal-tar derivative, the resulting dyes have been known ever since as "aniline dyes," even though they now also come from other compounds. After Perkin's break-

12

through, other aniline dyes were soon discovered and the synthetic dye industry was born, causing the rapid bankruptcy of the then-flourishing natural dye industry. The greatest progress in the development of synthetic dyes came after World War II, and today there are more than 2,000 dyes produced by many different companies.

The Textile Dye Industry

The dye industry is now one of the largest chemical industries in the world, with many companies manufacturing a variety of dyes specifically for certain products such as foods, cosmetics or textiles. The fiber artist, however, is only concerned with those particular dyes used for textiles.

European companies, particularly Swiss, German and British, dominate the textile dye industry today; many companies in the U.S. no longer find it profitable to compete. None of the chemical companies, however, manufacture dyes specifically for the home dyer. They are interested primarily in the industrial user, who purchases the dyes in large quantities. As a result, it has been necessary for the home dyer to adapt the methods used by industry into procedures that can be used safely and conveniently in the home.

Like most inventions or discoveries, new dyes are patented by the company responsible for their development. In return for full disclosure of the discovery, the company is given a specified period during which no other company may produce the dye. When the patent expires, however, any company that wishes may also manufacture the dye. Since a large number of dyes were developed years ago, many patents have expired, and today various companies are marketing the same dyes under their own brand names.

This practice can be compared to that of the drug companies, each of which markets a particular antibiotic under its own brand name. However, by knowing the generic name for the antibiotic (for example, tetracycline) the purchaser can determine which brands are actually the same chemically. It is important for the dyer to know whether two different companies' dyes are chemically identical since not all distributors carry the same brands. This makes it possible to use various companies' dyes and still achieve the same color mixing results. Also, dyers working with different brands that are chemically identical can share their formulas. For this reason the dyer should be aware of the generic names for the dyes being used. This information may be found in the *Colour Index*.

The Colour Index

The *Colour Index*, available in a few large city and university libraries, is a multivolume joint publication of the Society of Dyers and Colourists in Great Britain and the American Association of Textile Chemists and Colorists (AATCC) in the United States. It provides a dual classification of all dyes, grouping them according to their usage classes and also according to their chemical structure. In addition, all dyes are listed by their commercial names in a separate volume.

The dyes in Volumes 1 to 3 are arranged according to their usage class — such as acid dyes or reactive dyes — and are listed by their generic names. The generic name is referred to as the "Colour Index Name" or "C.I. Name." Technical information including fastness properties is found for each generic dye in these volumes.

Volume 4, on the other hand, lists dyes numerically according to chemical structure. A five-digit number referred to as the "Colour Index Constitution Number" or "C.I. Number" is given to each dye, and a particular series of numbers is reserved for each group of dyes having a similar chemical structure. For example, C.I. numbers 11000-19999 are given to those dyes that contain chemical groups known as monoazo compounds. The structural formula, method of preparation, chemical and physical properties, references and patent number is given for each C.I. Number. In Volume 4, dyes which are chemically related but belong to different usage classes may be found together.

The commercial names for the various dyes are found in Volume 5. The information is arranged in two ways: a C.I. Generic Names Index, in which the commercial name plus the manufacturer is listed for each generic dye (arranged by class), plus a Commercial Names Index, in which the dyes are listed alphabetically by commercial name. Volume 6 is a supplement and contains chemical, application and fastness information on dyes released since the Third Edition was published in 1971.

Table 2, using information from Volume 5 of the *Colour Index*, illustrates how the dyer can tell whether two brands of dyes are chemically the same. The Intracid dye Fast Yellow 2GC and the

TABLE 2

COMMERCIAL DYES BY GENERIC NAME

COMMERCIAL NAME	CLASS	MFR.	C.I. GENERIC NAME	C.I. NUMBER
INTRACID	Acid	CKC*		
Fast Yellow 2GC	Acid	CKC	C.I. Acid Yellow 17	18965
Red 2G	Acid	CKC	C.I. Acid Red 1	18050
Blue A	Acid	CKC	C.I. Acid Blue 7	42080
ERIO	Acid	CGY**		
Yellow 2G	Acid	CGY	C.I. Acid Yellow 17	18965
Floxine 2GN	Acid	CGY	C.I. Acid Red 1	18050
Blue 4GL	Acid	CGY	C.I. Acid Blue 25	62055

*CKC: Crompton & Knowles
**CGY: Ciba-Geigy

Erio Yellow 2G dye both possess the generic name Acid Yellow 17, which means they are identical chemically. The same is true of the two red dyes listed. The two blue dyes, however, have different generic names, which means they are not the same. If the dyer substituted one blue dye for the other, color mixing results would be altered.

What's in a Name?

The name given to a particular dye by the manufacturer, such as "Erio Yellow 2G" or "Procion Red MX-8B," is designed to convey certain information. To begin with, the particular brand name tells what class of dyes is involved, which in turn indicates the properties of the dye and how it should be used. A different brand name is used for each specific dye class. "Erio," for example, is Ciba-Geigy's brand name reserved for all leveling acid dyes. The brand name "Procion" is used by ICI for all its fiber-reactive dyes for cellulose. The letters "-nyl" attached to the brand name indicate a dye specifically designed for use with nylon. Ciba-Geigy's brand name "Erionyl" is an example.

With the fiber-reactive class of dyes, code letters are used after the brand name to indicate a particular type of reactive group.

This is necessary because while the same chemical reaction occurs with all the reactive groups, the conditions under which it takes place vary with the type and number of reactive groups involved. Some groups react more slowly than others and require

TABLE 3

CODE LETTERS USED FOR FIBER-REACTIVE DYES

FIBER-REACTIVE BRAND NAME	CODE LETTERS	TEMPERATURE OF DYE REACTION
Procion	MX	105° F
Procion	H	175° F
Procion	H-E	175° F
Cibacron	F	105° F

the use of heat for the reaction to take place. This information is important to the dyer because it indicates both the dyeing procedure that should be followed when applying the dye and the application process for which the dye is best suited.

The name of a dye is also designed to give information about its specific attributes. Hue is the most important, with the name of the dye color, such as "red" or "blue," following the brand name. Equally important is the position of the hue on the color wheel to distinguish it from dyes of similar hue; any hue may shade toward the color on either side of it. Red, for example, may be bluish red or reddish yellow, and blue can lean toward its yellow

TABLE 4

COLOR SUFFIX LETTERS SHOWING THE DIRECTION

COLOR	SUFFIX LETTER	HUE DIRECTION
Yellow	G	toward green
	R	toward red
Red	G	toward yellow (from the German *gelb*)
	B	toward blue
Violet	R	toward red
	B	toward blue
Blue	R	toward red
	G	toward green

neighbor (greenish blue) or its red neighbor (reddish blue). This information is given after the color name in the form of code letters to indicate in which direction the color leans. The degree of departure from the pure hue color is often indicated by a number (the higher the number, the greater the "leaning"). For example:

"Intracid Red 2G" means a level dyeing acid wool dye manufactured by Crompton & Knowles, red in hue with a moderate yellow cast.

"Procion Red MX-8B" refers to a fiber-reactive dye produced by ICI belonging to the MX series, red in hue with a strong bluish cast.

Additional code letters are used with the above suffixes to indicate technical features or special use of the dye. At times different companies use the same letter to convey separate meanings. A few of the more common uses of code letters are listed below.

L usually means "fast to light" as in "Intracid Fast Red BL."

N usually signifies "new," and often refers to an improved dye that is replacing a former dye.

Conc is always used to indicate a higher strength standard.

P may mean several things, including "suitable for textile printing," or "fast to perspiration."

S also has many meanings, including "soluble," "sweatfast" or "specially applicable to silk."

What Is a Dye?

Before examining the many classes of dyes available to the fiber artist, it is important to have a basic understanding of what a dye is. The dictionary defines *dye* as any substance used to color something, while a *dyestuff* is any material used as or yielding a dye, so the two terms can be used interchangeably. For a dye to be useful, it must also be able to color something more or less permanently.

Most people who use natural dyes are familiar with some plant extract that produces a beautiful color but, unfortunately, is "fugitive"—that is, fades easily. Such dyes are of little value.

A typical dye molecule is composed of different chemical groups, each responsible for a particular property of the dye, including the chromophore, the auxochrome and the solubilizing group. The *chromophore* is the color-producing portion of the dye molecule. It is composed of chemicals that possess

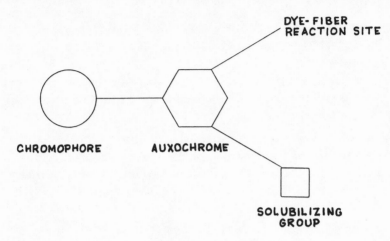

1. Typical dye molecule.

properties which allow light to be selectively absorbed, resulting in a particular color being seen by the eye. A different chemical group is responsible for each color. The *auxochrome* influences the intensity of the color that is seen; again, various chemical groups control this property. It also provides the site at which the dye chemically bonds with the fiber. And, finally, the *solubilizing group* allows the dye molecule to be water-soluble so that it is capable of reacting with the fiber in a waterbath. As with the other two parts of the dye molecule, different chemical groups can be used to achieve this. Chemicals used to alter conditions of the dye reaction—for example, to raise or lower the pH—are referred to as *dyeing assistants*.

The properties exhibited by a particular dye are determined by the chemical groups that are combined to make up the dye molecule. Chemical incompatibilities prevent certain molecular combinations from occurring, which explains why it is not always possible to produce a certain color of dye or a dye of high intensity. Compromises must be made.

Fastness Properties of the Dyes

The *fastness* of a dye refers to its ability to resist fading following application. Every dye that is produced undergoes a series of tests by its manufacturer to determine its fastness to such conditions as washing, sunlight and perspiration. The conditions for these tests may be devised by one or more of various standards organizations, including the International Organization for Standardization (ISO) and the American Association for Textile Chemists and Colorists (AATCC); or the manufacturer may have its own methods for assessing fastness. In any case, most companies use an internationally-agreed-upon numerical grading system in rating the fastness properties of their dyes.

While the industrial user is concerned with the fastness properties of the dyes under a variety of conditions, the home dyer is mainly interested in how well the dye holds up when the fiber is washed and exposed to sunlight. The degree of fading that occurs when a dyed sample of fabric is washed in hot water is measured from 1 to 5, with 5 denoting "no change" when compared to a control sample. Any significant change in shade (for example, becoming bluer) is also noted. The temperature used for the washing test depends on the class of dyes being evaluated. For example, the premetallized dyes, which are known for very good washfastness, are tested at 140° F, while the leveling acid dyes are tested at lower temperatures (usually 105°F), since they are known to fade in hot water. The fiber-reactive dyes, however, are noted for excellent washfastness, so are tested at temperatures as hot as 205° F.

A xenon lamp, which simulates sunlight, is used in the dye industry to more quickly determine the amount of fading that will occur when samples of dyed fabric are exposed to it. Test results are rated from 1 to 8, with 8 indicating no color change and, therefore, a high degree of fastness. Dyeings of various strengths are tested; the paler tint of a color often receives a lower rating than the same color tested at full strength.

While most dyes in a particular class may receive an "acceptable" rating for a particular fastness test, fastness can vary with the individual chromophore, so each individual dye should also be considered. For example, as a class the leveling acid dyes are noted for good lightfastness. The chromophores responsible for producing the colors turquoise, green and pink, however, are affected by sunlight to a greater degree than the other chromophores, so that these colors fade significantly. These leveling acid dye colors should be avoided when lightfastness is important, as, for example, in a tapestry that will be exposed to bright sun.

Dye Groups and Classes

The majority of textile dyes produced are not important to the home dyer since they are not suitable for use because of dangerous chemicals, expensive equipment or complicated procedures. Only those dyes that are easy and safe to use in the home environment and produce satisfactory results are considered in this book. But even with these restrictions there are still a large number of dyes that can be used.

These dyes, as shown in Table 5, can be divided into four groups based on how they attach to the fiber. Each group in turn is made up of one or more dye classes.

Two factors must be considered when deciding whether a

TABLE 5

FOUR GROUPS OF DYES

METHOD OF ATTACHMENT	DYE CLASS	APPLIED TO	BRAND NAME EXAMPLES
Covalent bond	Fiber-reactive dyes	Cellulose, silk Wool	Procion Cibacron Hostalan
Ionic bond	Acid dyes Basic dyes Metal-complex dyes Chrome mordant dyes	Wool, silk, nylon Acrylic, modacrylic Wool, silk, nylon Wool, nylon	Erio (Kiton*) Astrazon Irgalan (Cibalan*) Eriochrome
Physical surface sources	Direct dyes Disperse dyes	Cellulose, silk Acetate, nylon, polyester	Chlorantine Dispersol
Mechanical bonding or pigmentation	Vat dyes Azoic or Naphthol dyes	Cellulose, silk Cellulose	Indigo Cibanone Brentamine Fast Color Salts and Brenthol Coupling Agents

*old brand name

specific class of dyes can be used with a certain fiber: 1) a compatible bonding mechanism between the dye and fiber molecules and 2) the dyeing assistants or chemicals that are used to aid the process. Because of the molecular differences between the synthetic fibers, the protein fibers (for example, wool), and the cellulose fibers (for example, cotton), no one class of dyes is able to react with all the fibers. Generally those dyes that react with the protein fibers will not work with the cellulose fibers and vice versa, while the synthetic fibers often require special dyes because of their chemical structures. Even if a dye is able to attach to the fiber molecule it may not be usable if it requires harmful dyeing assistants. (The strong alkali used with the vat dyes, for example, is destructive to wool.) The chemical structure of the dye, the fiber and the chemicals used to assist the dye reaction must all be considered when choosing a class of dyes.

Fiber Chemistry

Of all the many fibrous materials nature has produced, only a few are useful as textile fibers. While willow saplings and bear grass can be used for weaving baskets, they don't work very well for weaving or knitting material. Wool, on the other hand, is ideally suited for weaving cloth and knitting. Basically, the main difference between those fibers that can be used for textiles and those that can't is the ability to be spun into yarn.

The ability of a fiber to be spun into a yarn is primarily determined by two things: 1) the structure of the fiber and 2) its chemical composition. These properties are also important to the dyer because they influence the dye reaction. A typical dye-fiber reaction is the result of some sort of chemical attraction between certain reactive groups on the dye molecule and reactive groups on the fiber molecule. And it is the chemical makeup of the fiber which determines the type of reactive groups that will be present.

The natural textile fibers can be classified into three groups based on their chemical composition: protein, cellulose and mineral fibers. (Mineral fibers, of which asbestos is the only naturally-occurring example, are not commonly used by the home fiber person and will not be considered here.) The following table lists the more typical examples that are found in each of the two other groups.

TABLE 6

IMPORTANT PROTEIN AND CELLULOSE TEXTILE FIBERS

PROTEIN	CELLULOSE
Wool	Cotton
Silk	Linen
Alpaca	Jute
Mohair	Ramie
Angora	Hemp
	Sisal
	Rayon*

*a manufactured cellulose fiber

Knowledge of the chemical structure of the fiber is also useful to the dyer in predicting how readily the fiber can absorb the dye. A typical textile fiber is composed of identical groups of molecular units joined together in an orderly way to form long chains. These long chains are referred to as *polymers,* with the individual molecular units called *monomers.*

2. Amorphous area of fiber (left). Crystalline area of fiber (right).

The pattern of arrangement of the polymers within the fiber is especially important in determining how readily a dye is absorbed. In some portions of the fiber these polymer chains are arranged quite randomly, looping and coiling around each other. These are the *amorphous areas* of the fiber. In other parts of the fiber, referred to as the *crystalline areas*, the polymer chains line up in almost parallel precision. The neatly aligned polymers serve as a sort of barrier to the penetration of liquids, preventing the dye from freely entering. As a result, the highly crystalline areas are not easily dyed. In contrast, areas of low crystallinity in the fiber, where the polymer chains are haphazardly arranged, are easily penetrated by liquids, causing the fiber to swell and thus allowing maximum absorption of the dye.

Each textile fiber differs from every other in the number and chemical structure of the monomers that make up the polymer chain, the number and type of reactive units found on the chain and the arrangement of the polymers in the fiber. These features are unique for each fiber. Properties of each fiber that influence the dye reaction are discussed in the following sections. Physical characteristics that affect the dyeing operation are also mentioned.

The Protein Fibers

Protein fibers, like all forms of protein, are formed of amino acids, of which there are approximately twenty-six. Almost all of these occur in the various protein fibers but in different proportions and arrangements. This explains why the protein of wool is different from the protein of alpaca.

Most protein fibers are the result of animal hair growth and react similarly in the dyepot. Some variation occurs, however, in the depth of color and exact shade achieved. Silk differs from all the other protein fibers because it is a secretion rather than a hair growth. It also reacts somewhat differently from the other fibers, and is discussed in a separate section for this reason.

The Chemistry of Wool

The wool fiber is composed of the protein *keratin*. This is a complex protein molecule made up of eighteen different amino acids combined to form what is called a *polypeptide chain*. These chains are joined or bridged at different points by various amino acids that, because of electrically opposite charges, are able to attract and hold each other. Chemically this bridge can be represented as ^-OOC-Wool Molecule-NH_3^+ with the positive part (NH_3^+) contributed by one amino acid and the negative part (^-OOC) coming from another amino acid. The particular amino acids themselves are not important. What is important is that two

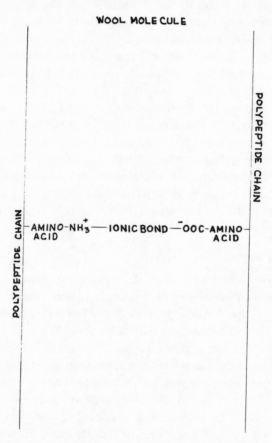

3. Diagram of wool molecule showing ionic bonding between two amino acids of opposing charges.

amino acids of opposing charges occur opposite each other so that this joining can take place. This type of chemical attraction is called *ionic bonding,* with a salt link or bridge being formed. The areas of the fiber where these salt linkages occur are where the dye molecules can attach.

In addition to those amino acids which are ionically bonded there are other amino acids (cysteines) which are joined by a much stronger type of chemical bond (a covalent bond) and are responsible for keeping the wool molecule together (cysteine linkage). While these groups are not involved with the actual dye-bonding reaction, they can be affected by the chemicals used during a dyeing operation.

With strong alkalis, such as the sodium hydroxide used with the vat dyes, these bonds show appreciable damage in a short time, especially at high temperatures. Even mild alkalis such as ammonia and sodium carbonate (washing soda) cause a small amount of damage to the protein molecule, although they can safely be used at temperatures below 160° F.

Fortunately, these bonds show good resistance to damage by acids, since acids are commonly used in wool dyeing recipes. While prolonged boiling of wool with dilute acids would eventually destroy the protein bonds, the length of time the wool is actually exposed to acid during dyeing produces negligible damage. The wool should be washed afterwards, however, to remove the acid residue that could eventually rot the fiber.

These bonds are also weakened by bleaching and sunlight. This is why the tip end of a fleece, exposed to sunlight, will take the dye differently than will the root end of the fleece, located next to the body.

The protective outer layer or cuticle of the wool fiber also influences the dye reaction. Microscopically, the cuticle appears as a layer of overlapping scales. While this cuticle is one of the reasons why wool is so easily spun, it also is responsible for the felting of wool that occurs when heat, moisture and friction—typical dyebath conditions—are present. The cuticle also retards the penetration of liquids into the fiber. Heating reduces this resistance, but the dyer must be extremely gentle in moving the fiber in the waterbath to keep the scales from locking. Once this physical barrier has been passed, however, wool is easily penetrated by the dye, a result of the low crystallinity of the fiber.

The Chemistry of Silk

Silk differs somewhat from the other protein fibers in several important ways. First, rather than being a hair growth, it is the secretion product of the silkworm into a continuous filament. Although silk is composed of protein (called *fibroin*), which like the other protein fibers is made up of many different amino acids and contains the ^-OOC and NH_3^+ reactive groups, it also possesses the same reactive hydroxyl groups ($-OH$) found on cellulose fibers. These hydroxyl groups, however, occur on only

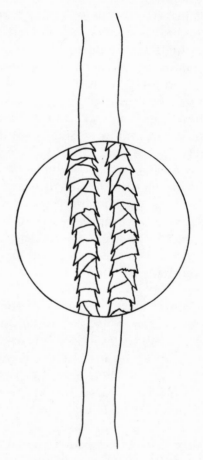

4. Wool fiber, when viewed through a microscope, appears as overlapping plates or scales.

one of the many amino acids which make up the silk protein, and are located in a portion of the fiber which is not as easily penetrated by the dye (high crystalline areas). This means that while silk can be dyed with both the protein and the cellulose dyes, less intense colors are possible with the latter.

With the acid dyes (the most commonly used dyes for protein fibers) silk behaves similarly to wool—with several important exceptions. First of all, fewer acid-combining sites (NH_3^+) occur on the silk molecule, which means that if both silk and wool are present in the same dyebath the silk will dye a lighter shade. Silk, however, does not contain the same protective coating (cuticle) that the wool fiber possesses, so it is able to react more quickly with the dye molecule at lower temperatures. As the temperature is raised towards boiling, however, the dye molecule is transferred back into the dyebath. This means that the colors of silk are more intense at lower than higher temperatures. Fortunately, silk

Comparison of the dyeing ability of leveling acid dyes on wool (on top in both photos) and silk. The fibers in the top photo were dyed a tertiary shade using a mixture of the three traditional acid primary dyes—Acid Red 1, Acid Yellow 17, and Acid Blue 45. The silk appears much lighter than the wool, indicating little dye uptake by the silk. In the lower photo, Acid Blue 7 (sapphire blue) was substituted for Acid Blue 45; Acid Yellow 23 (lemon yellow), for Acid Yellow 17; and Acid Red 73 (scarlet), for Acid Red 1. The silk is able to react chemically with these dyes, as indicated by the similar color of the two fibers.

is so highly reactive that it is not necessary to raise the temperature of the dyebath above 185° F. (This is fortunate, since boiling tends to reduce the strength and luster of silk, especially in the presence of acids.)

The tendency of the dye molecule to return to the waterbath as the temperature is raised is responsible for the poor washfastness of silk dyed with the leveling acid dyes. As long as silk is drycleaned, this is not a problem. If better washfastness is required, however, other classes of dyes, such as the 1:2 premetallized or the fiber-reactive dyes, can be used.

The behavior of silk with the leveling acid dyes differs from that of wool in one other important aspect. For certain chemical reasons, the silk fiber is unable to react with some of the leveling acid dye colors, including the majority of dyes used as the primaries. By substituting scarlet for red, lemon yellow for yellow and sapphire blue for blue, acceptable color mixing results can be obtained with the leveling dyes. The turquoise dye is able to react with silk, so there is no need for an alternative for this color.

The Chemistry of Nylon

Nylon, a synthetic polyamide fiber, can react with the acid dyes because its molecular structure contains the same NH_3^+ and ^-OOC ions found in protein fibers. These groups, however, occur only at the ends of the molecular chain, so there are fewer sites where the dye can attach. Even so, nylon has a high chemical affinity for the acid dyes, so that a given amount of dye will produce a more intense shade with nylon than with wool.

Acid Dye Chemistry

The acid dyes are the most important dyes used with the protein fibers because of their chemical affinity for these fibers. A general understanding of what is occurring during the dyeing process will help the dyer to better control the procedure and evaluate the results.

While all acid dyes contain acidic groups in their molecular structure, so do many other types of dyes (for example, mordant, direct, reactive). The term "acid" more accurately refers to the method of application: an acid is added to the dyebath, allowing the dye to chemically bond with the fiber. There are many types of acid dyes, each suited to specific dyeing situations and conditions of use. These are described in Chapter 3, "The Protein Fiber Dyes." All of these dyes, however, react at least partially in the same manner.

Water is an excellent solvent for many compounds, allowing them to "come apart" chemically. Chemicals that react this way in water are called *electrolytes*, and their various parts are called *ions*. All ions are either negatively or positively charged and are able to combine with other ions of opposite charge (opposites attract). This is what happens to the wool protein molecule in water. The bonds (salt links) which hold the oppositely-charged amino acids together ionize (come apart) in water and form positive (NH_3^+) and negative (^-OOC) ions. In this state they are free to attach to other oppositely-charged ions that may also be present in the dyebath.

TABLE 7

CHEMICAL REACTION OF AN ACID DYE WITH WOOL

W = wool molecule
D = dye molecule

$^-OOC\text{-}W\text{-}NH_3^+$ $+$ $H+$ $=$	The neutrally-charged wool molecule combines with the positively-charged H+ ions from the acid in the dyebath
$HOOC\text{-}W\text{-}NH_3^+$ $+$ $D-$ $=$	allowing the negatively-charged dye molecule to attach to the positive NH3+ ions on the wool molecule
$HOOC\text{-}W\text{-}NH_3D$	forming an ionic bond or salt link with the dye molecule.

During the dyeing procedure, an acid or acid-producing chemical is added to the dyebath. This results in the production of positive hydrogen ions (H^+), since by definition all acids form hydrogen ions in water. The dye, which has a negative charge, allows the positive ions from the acid to attach themselves to the negative portion of the wool molecule, which in turn allows the negative dye molecule to bond with the positive ions on the fiber. What is referred to as a *salt link* is formed between the wool molecule and the dye molecule, joining the two chemically.

With the leveling acid dyes, which are noted for their even results, these ionic bonds are easily broken and reformed. This process, which allows the dye to evenly distribute itself over the fiber, is called *leveling*. For the same reason, however, fibers colored with these dyes tend to fade when washed in hot water. It is not chemically possible to have both good leveling and good washfastness with these dyes.

Acid dyes that are noted for good washfastness such as the 1:2 premetallized dyes depend on special features of the dye molecule to produce increased bonding of the dye to the fiber. Unfortunately, these special features also reduce the ability of the dye to distribute itself evenly over the fiber. As a result, even dye results are difficult to achieve. Such dyes are best used to color loose wool (fleece) rather than yarns or fabrics.

The Chemistry of Cellulose

While the protein fibers are able to react with the acid dyes because of the presence of ionic bonding sites, the cellulose fibers lack these types of reactive groups and remain undyed with the acid dyes. Hence dyes which depend on a different type of bonding mechanism must be used with these fibers. In order to determine the chemical reactions of which cellulose is capable, we must first examine its molecular structure.

Cellulose is composed of the same chemicals that make up sugar, but its molecular structure is much larger and more complex. This is why sugar dissolves in water while cellulose remains unchanged. A glucose monomer, or unit composed of carbon, oxygen and hydrogen, is the basic building block of cellulose; many of these glucose units joined together form a cellulose polymer. These polymers in turn form bundles of molecular chains that then combine into groups which become the cellulose fiber. Thus, a cellulose fiber is a highly complex molecular structure composed of many similar glucose monomers.

Of importance to the dyer is the fact that each glucose monomer contains several chemically-reactive hydroxyl groups $(-OH)$ which serve as dye bonding sites. At each site on the cellulose fiber the hydroxyl group can either be removed and replaced by another chemical group supplied by the dye molecule or it can be modified by chemically removing the hydrogen so that the dye molecule reacts with the oxygen that remains. (These same hydroxyl groups are also able to react with water, which is why cellulose can absorb large amounts of moisture and still keep the wearer feeling cool.)

While there are many types of cellulose fibers, including cotton, linen, jute and viscose rayon (a manufactured cellulose fiber), they are all made up of the same chemical compounds, allowing them to react similarly with the cellulose dyes. Variations in physical structure, such as the presence of a protective outer coating or the amount of cellulose which makes up the fiber, will influence how readily and to what degree the dye will be absorbed. Experimentation is necessary to determine how a particular fiber will react. In general, the order of absorption (strongest values to weakest) will be as follows:

Viscose rayon (darkest value)
Mercerized cotton*
Linen
Unmercerized cotton (lightest value)

Fiber-Reactive Dye Chemistry

The fiber-reactive dyes are the most important class of dyes used with the cellulose fibers because of the type of bonding that occurs when they are used. As the name "fiber-reactive" suggests, the dye contains reactive groups which actually chemically join with the fiber, as opposed to the weaker type of ionic bonding that occurs with the acid dyes. The reactive dye-fiber union is achieved by means of a covalent bond, which involves electron sharing and is the strongest type of chemical bonding that can occur. In this case the sharing occurs between certain atoms in the reactive group on the dye molecule and the hydroxyl groups on the cellulose. As a result, the covalent bond between the dye and the fiber is quite strong, making it insoluble in water and giving these dyes very good washfastness.

While all fiber-reactive dyes are capable of forming this covalent bond, some types are able to do it more readily than others. This ability is determined by the number and the

---

*In the mercerizing process, the cotton fiber is treated with concentrated sodium hydroxide, a strong alkali. This treatment slightly increases the space between the molecular chains which make up the fiber, allowing the dye to be absorbed more readily. An added benefit of the process is increased strength and luster of the fiber.

chemical configuration of the reactive group(s) that are present on the dye molecule. Some groups contain molecules that are so highly reactive they are able to chemically bond with the fiber at room temperature. For this reason, they are often referred to as "cold"-type reactive dyes. Procion MX is an example. Other types are much slower in reacting and require the addition of heat to supply enough energy for the dye reaction to occur. These are the "hot"-type reactive dyes such as Procion H-E.

Obviously, then, the type of reactive dye being used will affect the dyeing procedure (heat or no heat). It is important for the dyer to understand the reactive nature of the dye being chosen because that determines how the dye should be handled and the most suitable dyeing conditions. This is because the same reactive dye groups which combine with the hydroxyl groups on the cellulose fiber also are capable of reacting in the same way with the hydroxyl groups in water $(H-OH)$. This reaction is known as *hydrolysis*. Once the dye molecule has reacted with the water molecule, it is no longer available to bond with the fiber and is wasted.

Highly reactive dyes hydrolyze (react with water) much more readily than the slower reacting types. This means, for example, that a highly reactive dye such as Procion MX cannot be stored in water for any length of time. Also, hydrolysis is accelerated under alkaline conditions. During the dyeing procedure an alkali (washing soda) is added to the dyebath to allow the dye-fiber reaction to occur. Any dye that is not chemically fixed by the fiber will hydrolyze quite rapidly. As a result, even though the dyebath may still appear colored it cannot be reused since there are no reactive sites remaining on the dye molecule to bond with the fiber. They are all tied up with the water.

When a reactive dye is used for *exhaust dyeing*, which involves immersing the yarn or fabric in a waterbath to which the dye has been added, it is important that the dye have a good affinity for the fiber. This property is referred to as *substantivity* or preference of the dye for the fiber. A dye with sufficient substantivity is readily adsorbed by the fiber so that the reaction with cellulose predominates over the reaction with water. (*Ad*sorbtion is adhesion of the dye to the fiber surface.) Dyes of low substantivity are better suited for *continuous dyeing* —a process in which the dye is directly applied to the fiber, as in textile printing, and does not depend on an affinity for the fiber. The types of reactive dyes that are suitable for exhaust dyeing and are available to the home dyer will be discussed in more detail in Chapter 4, along with the conditions for using them.

The substantivity of a dye is determined by the molecular size of the dye; a large dye molecule favors substantivity. All fiber-reactive dyes are made up of small, highly soluble molecules and, for this reason, none are highly substantive. (The fact that the reactive dye molecule is quite small allows the molecule to move easily about in the dyebath. This condition favors leveling and rapid dyeing.) Still, there is enough size variation among these small molecules to produce differences in substantivity. This property is also affected by conditions of the dyeing process, including the temperature of the dye reaction and the solubility of the dye. As the temperature and solubility increase, substantivity decreases. Therefore large quantities of salt are added during the dyeing procedure to reduce the solubility of the dye, thus increasing its substantivity.

3. The Protein Fiber Dyes

The Acid Dyes

The most commonly used dyes for wool are the acid dyes because of the chemical affinity that exists between the fiber and the dyes. The "acid" in the name refers to the fact that the dyes are salts of organic acids and require the use of an acid or an acid-producing compound in the dyebath as a dyeing assistant. For the chemical reasons explained in the preceding chapter, these dyes also are suitable for the other protein fibers, including cashmere, alpaca, mohair and silk, and for the synthetic fiber nylon. There is some variation, however, in how the dyes react with the different fibers and in the colors that are produced. Experimenting will help the dyer achieve satisfactory results.

Classes of Acid Dyes

The acid dyes can be divided into three classes according to their application and wetfastness properties: 1) *leveling dyes,* 2) *milling dyes,* 3) *super milling* or *fast acid dyes.* This classification also reflects the amount of acid used in the dyeing procedure: group 1 is known as the *strong acid dyes,* group 2, the *weak acid dyes,* and group 3, the *neutral acid dyes.*

Leveling Acid Dyes

The leveling acid dyes are the most important class for the home dyer of yarns and fabrics, and for this reason will be discussed in detail. To many dyers the brand name "Kiton" is synonymous with this class of dyes, even though Kiton dyes are no longer produced. Ciba, Ltd., was the manufacturer of this brand for many years. When Ciba merged with Geigy in the early

34

1970s, the Geigy brand name "Erio" was chosen to represent the dye series. Even so, because of the dyer's familiarity with the Kiton name, many distributors still list the leveling dyes in their catalogs as "Kiton Dyes." The leveling acid dyes used for the work done for this book were purchased from Cerulean Blue, Ltd. in

TABLE 8

SOME MANUFACTURERS OF LEVELING ACID DYES

COMPANY	BRAND NAME
Ciba-Geigy	Erio (Kiton)
Crompton & Knowles	Intracid
Sandoz	Sandolan
American Color and Chemical	Amacid

Seattle, Washington, under the catalog heading "Ciba Kiton Acid Dyes." The dyes sold, however, are actually from various manufacturers. As long as the dyer works with the same generic colors, the brand name is not important.

Principles of Leveling Acid Dyeing

The first phase of the dyeing procedure is intended to distribute the dye evenly throughout the fiber. As their class name suggests, the leveling acid dyes are noted for producing even, or level, dye results. Because the dyes are molecularly simple, they migrate easily in the dyebath. The negative acid dye molecule attaches to the positive sites on the wool fiber and then unattaches and refixes at another site, enabling the dye to become evenly distributed.

The process of leveling is aided by the addition of a *leveling agent* such as Glauber's salt (sodium sulfate). Glauber's salt promotes even dyeing by slowing down the rate at which the dye bonds with the fiber. It does this by forming ions in water which compete with the dye ions for the positive sites on the fiber. Eventually, however, the dye molecules are able to replace the Glauber's salt ions because of their greater binding force. During this phase, heat is applied to promote adsorption of the dye by the fiber. Glauber's salt produces its leveling effect only with the leveling acid dyes. It will produce the opposite effect—that is, accelerate the reaction rate—with the neutral acid dyes.

The second phase of the dye reaction involves the addition of an acid which produces an excess of hydrogen (H^+) ions and allows the dye to chemically bond with the fiber. Sufficient acid is required to create a strongly acidic dyebath (pH 2-3). Industrially,

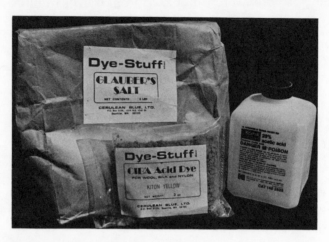

Acetic acid (vinegar) and Glauber's salt are the only chemicals needed with the leveling acid (Kiton) dyes.

this is obtained with sulfuric acid. Most home dyers use acetic acid or vinegar (a weak acetic acid solution) to achieve similar results with much more safety.

The temperature of the dyebath is then raised to boiling to promote more complete exhaustion of the dye as well as for the purpose of leveling the dyeing. In addition, without a sufficient heating period the dyes will not be properly fixed and will wash off.

Properties of the Leveling Acid Dyes

In addition to producing even results, the leveling acid dyes offer the home dyer many additional benefits. First, they produce very bright colors that mix well. It is possible to mix almost any other color using just the five primary hues—red, yellow, blue, magenta and turquoise. As a result, it is not necessary to stock a large number of dyes (although many other hues are available). This keeps inventory costs down. Leveling acid dyes are also economical in another way: they are quite concentrated. Just one ounce of dye can color from two to six pounds of fiber depending on the depth of shade desired. The home dyer can dye a large quantity of wool for very little money.

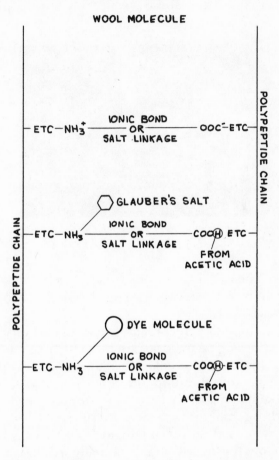

5. Diagram of wool molecule illustrating how the acetic acid allows the Glauber's salt and the dye molecule to chemically react with the positive amino acid (NH_3^+).

Washfastness and Lightfastness

The leveling acid dyes are known for moderate washfastness and very good lightfastness. As explained in the preceding chapter, it is not chemically possible to produce an acid dye with both good leveling ability and excellent washfastness. Because the dye molecule is small and able to migrate easily, it also can be removed during washing in hot water. Generally this is not a problem with wool and the other protein fibers, which are not normally subjected to frequent or hard washing. If the dyes are not washed in water above 105°F the fading problem is

One ounce of leveling acid dye powder can color this quantity of wool a medium shade for very little money.

minimized. The majority of leveling acid dyes receive a rating of 4-5 for washing tests performed at this temperature (5 means "no color change").

Resistance to fading in sunlight is considered very good with this class of dyes. The majority are rated 5-7 when tested at full strength (8 indicates "no color change"). Since this property is dependent on the chromophore, however, several exceptions should be kept in mind. These include turquoise, green and pink. If a yarn whose color formula for brown included red, yellow and turquoise was used in a wall hanging that was displayed by a bright window, the brown would gradually shade toward orange, because the turquoise would fade while the red and yellow remained essentially the same. This color change would be much worse than if the brown had just faded to a lighter value.

Milling Dyes

The milling dyes, also referred to as the weak acid dyes, are generally applied in a weakly acidic dyebath of between pH 5.2 and pH 6.2 (pH 7 is neutral). Although these dyes have much better washfastness than the leveling dyes, they unfortunately do not produce as even results, because the dye molecule is of a higher molecular weight and does not migrate as easily in the dyebath. Industrially, the milling dyes are used where good washfastness is the main consideration, such as in the production of felts. For the home dyer, however, their use is limited. In addition, the mixing ability of the individual dyes is poor.

TABLE 9

LIGHTFASTNESS AND WASHFASTNESS PROPERTIES OF THE LEVELING ACID DYES

C.I. NAME	LIGHTFASTNESS* (full strength)	WASHFASTNESS** (105° F)
Acid Red 1	5	5
Acid Yellow 17	6	5
Acid Blue 45 (Bright Blue)	4-5	4
Acid Violet 7 (Magenta)	4	4
Acid Blue 9 (Turquoise)	1	4-5
Acid Blue 7 (Sapphire Blue)	2	5
Acid Yellow 23 (Lemon Yellow)	4	5
Acid Red 73 (Scarlet)	6	5

*rated 1-8 (8 = "no change")
**rated 1-5 (5 = "no change")

Super Milling Dyes

The super milling dyes, also known as the fast acid dyes, are applied from a neutral or just slightly acid (pH 5.5 to pH 7) solution. They possess good lightfastness and wetfastness, and originally were used industrially where severe wet treatments were required in the fulling process of the wool fabric—a part of the milling operation. This explains why the term "milling" is applied to this dye class, although today it is used for other fibers and purposes.

Again, it is difficult to obtain even results with these dyes because of their high molecular weight (which is also responsible for their very good washfastness). Their application must be handled carefully. This is achieved by the use of an acid releasing salt (ammonium sulfate) in the dyebath, which upon heating slowly forms an acid (sulfuric acid) as the ammonia evaporates. (Ammonium sulfate is available at most garden stores, where it is sold as a fertilizer.) As the dyebath becomes acidic, the dye molecule is able to attach to the fiber at a controlled rate, resulting in more even dyeing.

Although the super milling dyes produce bright colors with very good washfastness, their popularity has declined since the introduction of the 1:2 premetallized dyes (described later in this chapter). This is because these dyes have the same desirable qualities and are generally less expensive to purchase.

Chrome Mordant Dyes

Mordants were originally associated only with the natural dyes. Because there is no chemical attraction between most natural dyes and the fiber, it is necessary to assist the reaction by applying a mordant to the fiber, which first bonds with the fiber and then in turn allows the dye to bond with the fiber-metal unit. Various metals such as chrome, aluminum, tin, copper and iron are used for this purpose, with the metal affecting the color produced.

It was discovered in the early 1900s that by mordanting certain acid dyes with chrome (the only metal then used industrially) it was possible to improve the washfastness of these dyes. The metal could be applied before, during or after the dyeing procedure; the name of the dye reflected the process used, for example, "afterchrome dyes." Once inside the fiber, the metal reacts with the dye to form an insoluble compound known as a "color lake." These compounds are responsible for the improved washfastness of the dyes.

While the mordant dyes are noted for very good washfastness, they have only fair lightfastness. In addition, the use of chrome produces characteristically dull colors.

The use of these dyes industrially has declined in recent years since the introduction of a more effective replacement, the metallized dyes. This is mainly because of the time-consuming and therefore expensive two-step process involved. There is also a disposal problem with chrome, since the metal is considered a pollutant. For the same reasons, the chrome mordant dyes are of limited importance to the home dyer.

Premetallized Dyes

To avoid the time-consuming two-step dyeing procedure necessary with the mordant dyes, industry developed a dye that allowed the mordanting and dyeing operations to be combined into a one-step process that could be applied using normal dyeing methods. This meant that it was necessary to combine the dye with the chrome into a compound that was also water-soluble. The premetallized dyes are the result of this research. The name indicates that there is a metal ion (chrome or cobalt) attached to the acid dye molecule. Like the chrome mordant dyes, the premetallized dyes have excellent washfastness plus characteristic dull colors.

There are two types of premetallized dyes, the 1:1 premetallized dyes and the 1:2 premetallized dyes, with the numbers referring to the ratio of metal atoms to dye molecules. The 1:1 dyes were the series originally developed. Because they involve a more expensive application process and the use of strong acids to convert the soluble dye-metal complex into an insoluble form within the fiber, they are not used much today either industrially or by the home dyer.

The 1:2 premetallized dyes (one metal atom to two dye molecules), which have been developed more recently, are much more important for both the industrial user and the home dyer.

TABLE 10

LIGHTFASTNESS AND WASHFASTNESS PROPERTIES OF THE 1:2 PREMETALLIZED DYES

C.I. NAME	COLOR	LIGHTFASTNESS* (full strength)	WASHFASTNESS** (140° F)
Acid Red 211	Bright Red	5-6	4-5
Acid Yellow 116	Yellow	6-7	5
Acid Blue 183	Brilliant Blue[1]	5-6	4
Acid Red 213	Bordeaux	7	5
Acid Blue 284	Navy	6-7	4
Acid Brown 19	Brown	7	5
Acid Black 62	Grey	6-7	4-5
Acid Black 107	Black	7-8[2]	5
Acid Yellow 127	Brilliant Yellow[1]	6	4-5

[1] super milling dye
[2] slight color change
*rated 1-8 (8 = "no change")
**rated 1-5 (5 = "no change")

These dyes have a high affinity for wool, which readily absorbs them in a neutral dyebath.

As with previously mentioned acid dyes, it is the large dye-metal molecule and the dye bonding mechanism which are responsible for superior washfastness. A large dye molecule is more easily trapped within the fiber and therefore less likely to return to the dyebath. Unfortunately, large dye molecules are not able to migrate as easily in the dyebath, which results in uneven dyeing. This means it is necessary to slow down the reaction process to allow the molecule to react with the fiber at a more controlled rate. As with the super milling dyes, this is accomplished by the use of an acid releasing salt (ammonium sulfate) that slowly produces an acidic dyebath as the ammonia evaporates. In this manner it is possible to achieve level dyeing.

In addition to very good washfastness, advantages of these dyes include ease of application and lack of fiber selectivity. The latter phrase means that if two fibers such as wool and silk are dyed together they will color similarly, which is not true with the leveling acid dyes. Also, if a blend of different types of wool is used, the dyes will cover evenly, which does not occur with many dye classes. The dyes also give excellent results with silk and even with some wool-synthetic blends.

To achieve brighter colors, the super milling dyes can be combined with the 1:2 premetallized dyes. Since both dyes require the same dyeing procedure, they can be used together in the dyepot. Distributors who carry the premetallized dyes for the home dyer often list both dyes under the heading "Premetallized dyes." Some dealers use the word "brilliant" before the color name to indicate that the dye is actually a super milling instead of a premetallized dye.

For the home dyer, the 1:2 premetallized dyes should be used whenever washfastness is important (for example, in the production of felt). Best results are obtained with fleece, which can then be blended during carding to even up the color, if desired.

The Basic Dyes

The *basic dyes* were the class of synthetic dyes developed by W. H. Perkin in 1856. The dyes are noted for producing colors of

TABLE 11

Dye Classes Used with Protein Fibers

	LEVELING ACID (Strong Acid)	MILLING (Weak Acid)	SUPERMILLING (Neutral)	1:1 PREMETALLIZED	1:2 PREMETALLIZED	CHROME MORDANT	BASIC
Washfastness	Very good to 105° F	Very good to 120° F	Very good to 120° F	Very good to 120° F	Very good to 140° F	Excellent to 140° F	Fair-good
Lightfastness	Very good (Except turquoise, green, pink)	Good	Good	Very good	Very good	Good	Poor
Brightness of Colors	Very bright	Bright	Bright	Dull	Dull	Dull	Very bright
Common Brand Names	Erio (Ciba-Geigy) Intracid (Crompton & Knowles)	Polar; Eriosin (Ciba-Geigy)	Irganol (Ciba-Geigy) Carbolan (ICI)	Neolan (Ciba-Geigy)	Irgalan (Ciba-Geigy) Intralan (Crompton & Knowles)	Eriochrome (Ciba-Geigy) Solochrome (ICI)	Astrazon (Verona Dyestuffs)
Comments	Most important class of dyes for wool yarns and fabrics.	Limited color selection. Difficult to produce even dyeing.	Requires use of acid-releasing salt. Useful for shade brightening of 1:2 premetallized dyes.	Requires strong acid for application.	Important dye class when good washfastness is required.	Difficult to achieve level dyeing. Chrome is a pollutant.	Limited usefulness for producing very bright colors on wool.

exceptional brilliance and intensity but of poor fastness, especially to light. Chemically they react similarly to the acid dyes (ionic bonding) except, that, as the name suggests, they have a positive charge—are basic instead of acidic. As a result, they chemically bond with the negative ($^-$OOC) rather than with the positive (NH_3^+) ions on the wool molecule. Acetic acid is used in place of Glauber's salt to slow the dye reaction rate so that even dyeing can be attained.

Although these dyes were originally used on wool, silk and cotton, mordanted with tannic acid, their most important usage today is with the acrylic fibers (Orlon, Creslan, Acrilan). This is because, though their fastness on natural fibers is quite poor, it is good with the acrylics. These dyes, however, are still important to the home dyer of wool when exceptionally brilliant colors are wanted. They also can be used quite effectively for dyeing such materials as reeds, raffia, grasses and barks because these materials contain tannic acid, which serves as a mordant and allows the dye to bond with the fiber.

All-Purpose, Union or Household Dyes

The *all-purpose, union* or *household dyes* are so called because they can be used equally effectively with both protein and cellulose fibers. These dyes are actually a mixture of the leveling acid dyes for wool and the direct dyes for cellulose. When they are used to dye a single fiber such as wool, only the portion of the dye which is specific for this fiber reacts, while the remainder of the dye is unused and is wasted. This is an expensive way to dye!

4. The Cellulose Fiber Dyes

The Fiber-Reactive Dyes — A Breakthrough in Cellulose Dyeing

The fiber-reactive dyes are the most important class of dyes for use with the cellulose fibers. They may also be used with silk (see The Chemistry of Silk, page 25). These dyes were introduced in 1956 by Imperial Chemical Industries, Ltd. (ICI) climaxing a

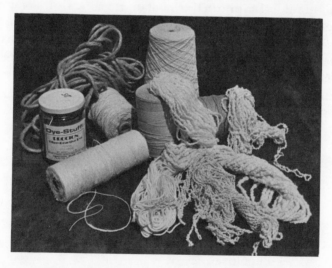

The fiber-reactive dyes can be used to color all the cellulose fibers including cotton, linen and jute, as well as rayon, a manmade cellulose, and silk, a protein fiber.

sixty-year period of research aimed at developing the ideal cellulose dye. Ironically, the fiber-reactive dyes had been known for some time, but research had been centered unsuccessfully around their use with wool. It was not until 1953 that two scien-

45

tists realized that these dyes were ideally suited for dyeing cellulose. Research emphasis was shifted, and in just three years the first reactive dyes for cellulose were on the market.

Prior to their discovery, four main groups of dyes had to be used for coloring cellulose: sulfur, direct, vat, and azoic or naphthol dyes. Each group possessed desirable properties but also had shortcomings in the key areas of shade range, method of use and fastness.

The sulfur dyes were characterized by hue weakness and the absence of any red dyes. The direct dyes also lacked hue strength and had poor fastness properties. Light- and washfastness were excellent with the vat dyes but, again, they exhibited hue weakness in the area of red dyes and required a skillful dyer for proper application. The azoic or naphthol dyes, on the other hand, offered an overabundance of red dyes but lacked greens. They were also difficult to use.

It is no wonder, then, that the introduction of the fiber-reactive dyes was heralded as one of the most important advancements in dye chemistry in recent times. Not only was a full range of hues possible, but these hues exhibited exceptional brilliance. In addition, the dyes were easy to use, possessed excellent washfastness and generally very good lightfastness, leveled well and were safe to handle. They were a dyer's dream come true.

Properties of the Fiber-Reactive Dyes
Bright colors
Good mixing ability
Even dyeing ability
Economical price
Fastness
Ease in using
Safety
Full color range

This list is almost identical to the one presented in Chapter 1 describing the ideal dye. The only disadvantage of this dye class concerns the removal of unfixed dye. Repeated rinsings and soaping are required to ensure complete removal so that no bleeding will occur during washing.

Fiber-Reactive Dye Series

While many brands of fiber-reactive dyes are being produced, only those currently available to the home dyer will be considered here. The "cold" series Procion MX dyes are the type most dyers are familiar with; however, "hot" type Procion dyes are also available. A "cold" series produced by Ciba-Geigy can also be purchased by the home dyer.

"Cold" type reactive dyes typically possess two highly reactive groups on the dye molecule that are capable of forming covalent bonds with the hydroxyl groups on the cellulose fiber. Procion MX (ICI) is an example of this type of reactive dye. Unfortunately,

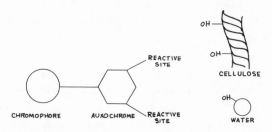

6. Typical cold type fiber-reactive dye molecule. The two reactive sites on the molecule are capable of forming covalent bonds with the hydroxyl groups on either cellulose or water.

the highly reactive nature of this dye also allows it to easily form covalent bonds with the hydroxyl groups in water $(H-OH)$. This means that the dyes cannot be stored for any length of time in solution.

Because there were hydrolysis problems during textile printing with the highly reactive MX dyes—the dye bled outside the pattern areas—ICI made efforts to develop a series with reduced reactivity. The result of this research was a much slower-reacting dye, which was named Procion H. By replacing one of the two highly reactive groups on the dye molecule with an unreactive group, dye chemists greatly improved the stability of the dye in water. An added benefit was that the unreactive group often increased the solubility of the dye, making the removal of any unreacted hydrolyzed dye following the dyeing process much easier. This change in the dye molecule, however, also reduced its reactivity, requiring a higher temperature for the dye reaction to proceed.

Although Procion H dyes were originally developed for continuous dyeing purposes, some are also suitable for exhaust dyeing. However, the Procion H-E dyes, a more recent development by ICI, were specifically developed for exhaust dyeing. (The "E" stands for exhaust.) Like the H dyes, the H-E dyes are slow-reacting, requiring the use of heat for the dye reaction to occur. The H-E dyes possess a larger dye molecule than either the Procion H or the Procion MX dyes, which improves their substantivity. Also important is their ability to fix or chemically bond a large percentage of the dye that is adsorbed by the fiber.

The high fixation potential of these dyes makes them less sensitive to variables in dyeing conditions such as the quantity of water and the concentration of salt used in the dyebath. Also, because of the high percentage of the dye that is bonded, these dyes are economical to use; little dye is wasted and the color yield is very high. In addition, this dye series is compatible with the Procion H series (both follow the same dyeing procedure), allowing certain Procion H dyes such as turquoise (a color unavailable in the H-E series) to be used to extend the color range.

The Cibacron F dyes, introduced in 1979, are Ciba-Geigy's version of the "cold" type reactive dyes. The "F" stands for fluorine, the type of atoms used in the reactive group on the dye molecule. While these dyes are considered highly reactive, they are not as reactive as the MX dyes. For this reason, their stability in water is very good.

Individual dyes possessing similar properties were deliberately chosen for this series, ensuring like behavior in the dyepot. This means that dyeing conditions do not have to be altered to accommodate the requirements of a particular dye, as is sometimes the case with the MX dyes. The dyes in the Cibacron F series are of low-to-moderate substantivity but, because they can be used at low temperatures, they can be used for exhaust dyeing (substantivity increases as temperature decreases). A result of their lower substantivity is that unreacted dye is easier to remove. (It should be noted that as long as the proper washing procedure is followed, unreacted dye can be completely removed from any of the dye series.)

The selection of a particular reactive dye series depends on the needs of the dyer and the requirements of the process. While the "cold" type reactive dyes are more convenient to work with, there are times when a "hot" type may give better results. For example,

TABLE 12

PROPERTIES OF THE FIBER-REACTIVE DYES

BRAND	PROCION MX	PROCION H	PROCION H-E	CIBACRON F
Temperature of dye reaction	105° F	175° F	175° F	105° F
Stock solution stability	1-2 weeks*	4-8 weeks*	4-8 weeks*	4-12 weeks*
Advantages	No heat required for dye reaction to occur.	Good for direct application methods.	High tolerance to variations in dyeing conditions. High color yield.	No heat required for dye reaction to occur.
Disadvantages	Short shelf life in solution.	Heat required for dye reaction to occur.	Heat required for dye reaction to occur.	Gaps in color range—no turquoise.
Uses	Batiking. Exhaust dyeing of yarns and fabrics.	Textile printing. Selected dyes suitable for exhaust dyeing with H-E series.	Exhaust dyeing of yarns and fabrics.	Exhaust dyeing of yarns and fabrics. Batiking. Textile printing.

*Loss of dye strength occurs with storage and is accelerated by increase in temperature and alkaline pH of water used to prepare stock solution.

tightly woven fabrics such as canvas duck or tightly plied yarns are more easily penetrated by the dye at high temperatures. The process of heating forces apart the fiber molecules, allowing the dye to circulate more freely. Of the cold type reactive dyes, the Cibacron F series may be kept in stock solution much longer than the MX dyes, but their color mixing range is not as extensive. Depending on the series chosen, certain trade-offs must be made.

Manufacturers and Distributors of Fiber-Reactive Dyes

While ICI was the first company to introduce the fiber-reactive dyes in 1956, with the brand name "Procion," other companies also hold patents for these dyes, based on their own methods for producing covalent bonding.

TABLE 13

SOME MANUFACTURERS OF FIBER-REACTIVE DYES

COMPANY	BRAND
ICI	Procion
Ciba-Geigy	Cibacron
Hoechst	Remazol
Verona Dyestuffs	Levafix

In addition, there are many distributors who purchase the Procion dyes, repackage them, and sell them under their own brand names. Examples of these include:

Dylon
Fabdec
Fibrec
Hi-Dye
Putnam Color Fast
Linda's Dyes

Some distributors also add salt and alkali to their dyes. These are two very inexpensive ingredients that the dyer can just as easily add as needed. The dyes are most economical if purchased in the pure dye form.

Principles of Exhaust Dyeing with the Reactive Dyes

For a reactive dye to be economically suitable for application by the exhaust method of dyeing, over 50 percent of the dye used must be chemically bonded to the fiber. This is dependent on the substantivity of the dye which, in turn, affects the degree of dye fixation. As stated in Chapter 2, the substantivity of a dye is the difference between the affinity of the dye for the fiber and its affinity for water and determines how much dye is adsorbed (exhausted) by the fiber. A dye with low substantivity, for example, is not sufficiently adsorbed by the fiber so that enough is present to be chemically bonded. This results in dye being wasted through hydrolysis.

The Procion MX, Procion H-E and Cibacron F dyes are suitable for exhaust dyeing because they possess a sufficient degree of substantivity and fixation. The Procion H series have a lower substantivity than the H-E series and are better suited to direct application techniques, although selected dyes can be used in conjunction with the Procion H-E series to extend the color mixing range. Dyes from various series, however, can only be used together if their dyeing procedures are similar. For example, the "hot" type H-E dyes and the "cold" type Cibacron F dyes cannot be combined. Regardless of the application process, however, the principles of the dye reaction are the same.

The first principle of reactive dyeing is to get as much dye onto the fiber as possible. This is the *exhaust phase*, in which the dye is adsorbed by the fiber and becomes evenly distributed. Both good penetration and even distribution of the dye are necessary if reproducible color results are to be obtained.

Exhaustion is accomplished by the use of salt (table or Glauber's), which does two things. First, when mixed with the water in the dyebath it creates a salt-water solution in which the solubility of the dye is greatly reduced. This condition favors adsorption of the dye by the fiber. Second, the salt suppresses the negative surface charges on the fiber so the dye molecule can get close enough to move onto the fiber. Since the dye does not chemically bond with the fiber at this time, it has a chance to level.

Salt and washing soda are the only chemicals needed with the fiber-reactive dyes.

The amount of salt required varies with the particular dye series, but it is always increased as the amount of dye solution increases. A deep shade requires more salt than a pale shade. Without ample salt, the dye cannot be as completely adsorbed by the fiber and is wasted.

The amount of salt required also depends on the temperature of the dye reaction. In general, low-temperature dyes require less salt than dyes used at higher temperatures. This is because substantivity is also influenced by temperature. As the temperature increases, substantivity decreases or, in other words, the affinity of the dye for water increases as the temperature increases. This is mainly because the solubility of the dye increases with temperature just as, for example, more sugar can be dissolved in hot water than cold. To counteract this effect, more salt is used to reduce the dye's solubility, which then favors adsorption by the fiber. This explains why the hot type Procion H and H-E dyes require more salt during the dyeing procedure than the cold type Procion MX or Cibacron F dyes.

The second stage of the dyeing reaction is considered the *reactive* or *dye fixation phase.* An alkali (sodium carbonate) is added to the dyebath, which raises the pH and allows the dye

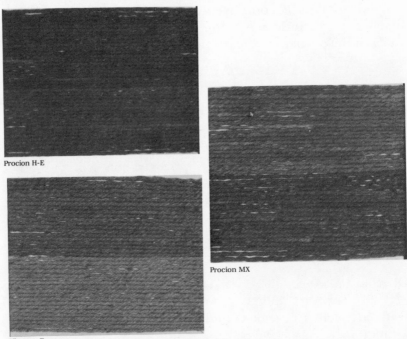

Procion H-E

Procion MX

Cibacron F

This series of photos compares the quantity of dye adsorbed by the fiber during dyeing (top band) to the amount that remains after the hydrolyzed dye has been removed by soaping (bottom band). The loss of dye is indicated by the lighter value of the bottom band. Note that the greatest color loss occurs with the Cibacron F dyes and the least with the Procion H-E dyes.

molecule to chemically bond with the fiber molecule. Once the pH of the dyebath has been raised, leveling can no longer occur. The dyer should be certain that the dye has been evenly distributed on the fiber prior to this point. Again, the amount of alkali varies with the dye series, but sufficient alkali is required to raise the pH above 10.5 with the Procion MX dyes and above 11 with the other series. The dye bonding reaction cannot properly occur at lower pH values, and the result is wasted dye. Also, the reaction period should not be cut short or the dye will not be properly fixed.

Unfixed Dye

While the whole purpose of the exhaustion and fixation phases is to bond as much dye as possible with the fiber, there is always a portion of dye that remains unfixed. This dye must be completely removed following the dyeing procedure to ensure depth of

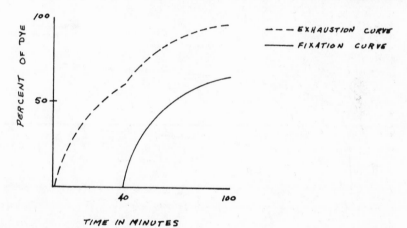

7. The exhaustion curve represents the total dye present on the fiber at the end of the dyeing process. The fixation curve shows the portion of the dye that has chemically reacted with the fiber. The difference between the two curves represents the portion of the dye that has hydrolyzed and must be removed by soaping to ensure wetfastness of the dye.

shade and fastness properties. Otherwise, bleeding will occur when the fiber is washed and the color will fade.

The unfixed dye remaining on the fiber is the result of hydrolysis. Ideally, the dye should react only with the fiber, but there is always some that bonds instead with the water. This hydrolyzed dye is still capable of exhausting onto the fiber, but it cannot be chemically fixed because there are no remaining sites on the dye molecule to chemically react with the fiber. The difference between the percentage of dye exhausted and the percentage fixed represents the amount of dye that has hydrolyzed and must be washed off.

Factors Influencing Removal of Unfixed Dye

Two factors influence the ease with which the unfixed dye can be washed off the fiber. The first has to do with substantivity. A dye of high substantivity would seem to be ideal since it would react mainly with the fiber and not with the water (that is, it would not be hydrolyzed). With a dye of high substantivity, however, it is more difficult to wash off the unfixed dye, because even though it has been hydrolyzed it is still adsorbed quite strongly by the fiber. This means that while most of a dye with high substantivity is

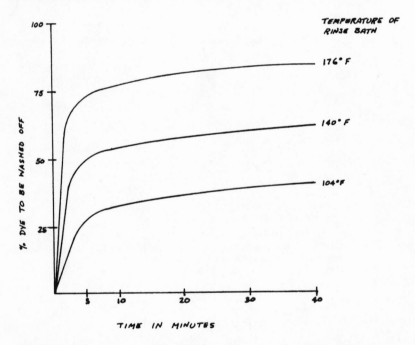

8. The effect of temperature and treatment time when unfixed dye is being washed off. This explains why several short rinsings in hot water are more effective than one long rinse.

chemically bound to the fiber and there is little unreacted dye to remove, this unreacted dye is more difficult to wash off. Con-

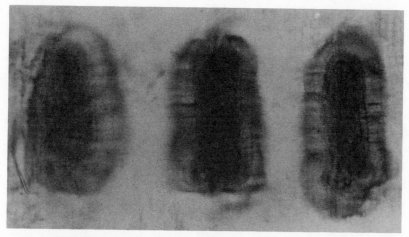

Procion MX   Procion H-E   Cibacron F

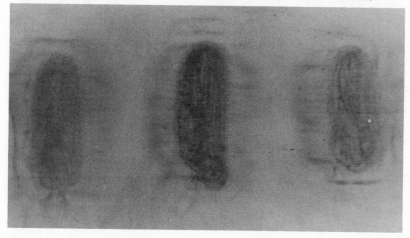

To determine if all of the hydrolyzed dye has been removed after a dyeing project, lay the wet fiber on an undyed fabric. Cover with a wet, undyed cotton fabric and dry-iron. Staining on the cotton fabric will indicate the presence of hydrolyzed dye. As the photographs indicate, a full ten minutes of soaping at the boil is necessary to remove all of the hydrolyzed dye for all of the reactive dyes tested. The top photograph shows fiber that was thoroughly rinsed under cold running water but had no soaping. Fiber in the bottom photograph was thoroughly rinsed under cold running water, soaped at the boil for five minutes and rinsed in hot water. Had the fiber had the same thorough cold-water rinsing and soaped at the boil for ten—rather than five—minutes before the hot-water rinsing, the second photograph would be white: no staining would show.

versely, a dye of low substantivity is more easily removed but there is a much larger percentage to be washed off.

The second factor affecting unfixed dye removal concerns *dye diffusion*, or the ease with which the dye molecule can move about. Rapid diffusion favors dye removal. The rate of diffusion is dependent on the temperature of the bath and the type of cellulose. Mercerized cotton allows the highest diffusion, followed by unmercerized cotton and viscose rayon. Also, the rate of diffusion is increased as the temperature is raised. Put simply, unfixed dye is most easily removed from mercerized cotton, and at high temperatures.

The unfixed dye is removed by first thoroughly rinsing the fiber, soaping it, then rinsing again. The purpose of the first rinsing is to remove all of the salt. Cold water is adequate for this purpose. As long as the salt remains on the fiber it is not possible to remove the unfixed (though hydrolyzed) dye because it remains adsorbed by the fiber.

Once all of the salt is washed off, the unfixed dye becomes more soluble and can be removed by soaping the fiber with detergent at very hot temperatures. Synthrapol, the "miracle" detergent, aids in the removal of this dye, although detergents commonly used for *scouring* (washing) fibers can also be used. Following soaping, the fiber is rinsed again to remove the dye and soap residues. Several short rinsings are preferable to one long rinsing because the unfixed dye tends to reach an equilibrium between the amount of dye in the bath and the amount left on the fiber. Thus, prolonged rinsing is ineffective (graph, page 54).

Fastness Properties

The excellent washfastness of the fiber-reactive dyes is the result of the type of chemical bonding that occurs (see Chapter 2, Fiber-Reactive Dye Chemistry). Lightfastness, however, is dependent on the particular chromophore; while it is generally considered to be very good for this class of dyes, the individual dye must also be examined.

Safety Considerations

While the fiber-reactive dyes are considered quite safe for home use, no chemicals should be handled carelessly. The dyes are considered "nontoxic" since they contain no known carcinogens, but care should be taken to avoid breathing the dust, a precaution that should be observed with any fine dust-producing substance. (With proper handling no dust should be created, and once the dyes are in stock solution the problem no

TABLE 14

LIGHTFASTNESS AND WASHFASTNESS PROPERTIES OF THE FIBER-REACTIVE DYES

BRAND	DYE NAME	LIGHTFASTNESS 1 (Medium Depth of Color)	WASHFASTNESS 2 (205° F)
Procion MX	Turquoise MX-G	6	4
	Blue MX-2GA (Navy)	3-4	4
	Blue MX-R	6	4-5
	Red MX-8B (Fuchsia)	4	5
	Red MX-5B	4	4
	Scarlet MX-G	3-4	3-4
	Scarlet MX-BRA	4	4
	Scarlet MX-BA	3-4	5
	Yellow MX-8G (Brilliant yellow)	4	5
Procion H-E	Turquoise H-A3	4-5	4-5
	Blue H-ERD	5	4-5
	Navy H-ER	4	5
	Red H-E3B	4	4-5
	Yellow H-E6G	4-5	5
	Green H-E4BD (Blue-green)	4-5	5
Cibacron F	Blue F-R	5-6	5
	Navy F-2R	5	5
	Red F-B (Fuchsia)	4	5
	Scarlet F-3G	4	4-5
	Yellow F-G	5-6	5
	Yellow F-3R (Golden yellow)	5	5

1 Rates are 1-8 (8 = "no change")
2 Rates are 1-5 (5 = "no change")
3 Procion H series, used with H-E series to extend color mixing range.

longer exists.) In addition, the fiber-reactive dyes are treated to minimize the formation of dust. The dyer should be aware, however, that cases of respiratory allergy have occurred among persons who have inhaled the dust over a long period of time. A face mask can be worn to minimize the problem.

As when working with any of the dyes, rubber gloves should be worn to prevent "rainbow hands." Some people with sensitive skin can also develop an allergic reaction to the dyes. Keep the hands out of the dyepot!

Fiber-Reactive Dyes for Wool

Fiber-reactive dyes specifically designed to be used with wool are also available. These dyes contain reactive groups that are capable of forming covalent bonds with certain amino acid and hydroxyl groups in wool. (The reactive dyes for cellulose possess reactive groups that bond only with the hydroxyl groups of cellulose and water.) Reactive wool dyes are mainly used to produce bright shades when better washfastness properties are required than can be obtained with acid wool dyes. Typical industrial situations include the dyeing of carpet fibers, which are subjected to frequent shampooing, and of wool fabrics that have been specially treated so they can be machine-washed. For the home dyer, the dyeing of wool for felting is an important usage.

In contrast to reactive dyes for cellulose, the reactive dyes for wool do not hydrolyze because the reaction occurs under near-acid-to-neutral conditions. One type of reactive wool dye available to the home dyer acts as an acid dye below temperatures of 185°F so that, with very slow heating, leveling can occur. Once the temperature climbs above 185°F, however, covalent bonding occurs and leveling is no longer possible. This means the dyes must be handled carefully to produce even results.

While the fiber-reactive dyes for wool will never replace the leveling acid dyes for most wool dyeing because of the special handling to achieve even dyeing and their higher manufacturing cost, they are valuable to the home dyer who needs bright shades with excellent washfastness. The lack of bright colors is a serious shortcoming with the 1:2 premetallized dyes.

Other Classes of Dyes for Cellulose

While the fiber-reactive dyes are ideally suited for most cellulose dyeing, there are occasions where other classes of dyes are needed. For example, a project may require superior lightfastness, or a particular shade not possible with fiber-reactive dyes.

These other dye classes include vat, azoic or naphthol, and direct dyes. An overview of these three classes is presented here to give the dyer an idea of their properties and potential for use. All are suited to exhaust dyeing and can be used in stock solution.

Vat Dyes

The vat dyes are among the fastest dyes known—that is, they have excellent resistance to fading in both sunlight and washing. ("Fastness" has nothing to do with the speed of the reaction.) They are also some of the oldest dyes known to man. Indigo is a classic example. The term "vat" refers to the vessel originally used for fermenting the indigo leaves, a process used to remove the oxygen. Today chemicals are used to accomplish the same result. While vat dyes originally came from only natural materials, today they are also synthetically produced. The synthetic vat dyes have been in use since the beginning of the 1900s.

The exceptional fastness properties of the vat dyes are due to the large dye molecule becoming trapped inside the fiber molecule rather than to a chemical reaction between the fiber and the dye. In its natural state the dye molecule is insoluble in water. Treatment with a *reducing agent* (a chemical that removes oxygen), however, converts it into a form which is soluble in water that has been made alkaline by the addition of sodium hydroxide. In this state the dye can be applied to the fiber in a waterbath. A natural affinity of the dye for cellulose causes it to adhere to the fiber. The dye is then oxidized by exposure to air, and the dye molecule is converted back to its original insoluble form. By this time, however, it is locked inside the fiber molecule and is not easily washed out because of its immense size.

It is interesting to note that the color of the reduced dye is different from the color produced when the dye is oxidized. Indigo, for example, turns from a yellow in the dyepot to a bright blue when exposed to air. The dyer feels somewhat like a magician.

While exposure to air is the common method for oxidizing the dye, one particular brand of vat dyes (Inko dyes) has been treated so that they are sensitive to light rather than to air. In this case, exposure to sunlight or even to artificial light will cause the dye to return to its insoluble reduced state.

Because the vat dyes depend on a mechanical rather than a chemical bonding, they could conceivably be used with any fiber. The strong alkali used as a dyeing assistant, however, is harmful to most protein fibers, and for this reason vat dyes are not recommended for these fibers. Silk is the one exception; it is less susceptible to damage by alkali and can successfully be colored with these dyes. The natural vat dyes such as indigo require a weaker alkaline solution and can be applied to protein fibers without appreciable damage.

While the vat dyes are noted for excellent fastness, their colors are muted. Also, the dyeing procedure is difficult to master and time-consuming. (Yarns dyed commercially with vat dyes are more expensive for this reason.) Most vat dyes available to the home dyer are available in paste rather than powder form, making them easier to work with and to measure.

Azoic or Napthol Dyes

The most important use of the azoic dyes is for the production of bright reds with excellent wash- and lightfastness on cellulose fibers. The Javanese batikers, especially, are noted for the brilliant reds of their work obtained with azoic dyes. Unfortunately, the dyeing procedure is complicated and requires the use of chemicals that are hazardous if mishandled.

The dyeing procedure requires the use of two different chemical compounds, a naphthol base and a fast-color salt—which are, however, applied separately. The fiber is first impregnated, usually through soaking, with the naphthol base to which an alkali (sodium hydroxide) has been added. The fiber is then wetted with the fast-color salt, which reacts immediately with the naphthol base to produce a color. By themselves, both compounds are colorless. It is only when they combine inside the fiber that a color is produced and the large dye molecule that is formed becomes trapped. While the dyes are difficult to work with, there is a sense of magic when the dyer pulls bright-colored cloth from a colorless solution.

Direct Dyes

The direct dyes have a strong affinity for cellulose fibers, although the chemical bonding that occurs is not particularly strong. For this reason, the washfastness of these dyes is not very good. The dyes, however, are easy to work with (salt is used as a dyeing assistant), producing colors that are somewhat muted. The one advantage these dyes have over the fiber-reactive dyes is better lightfastness for some colors. (While the fiber-reactive dyes as a class have very good lightfastness, there are some exceptions.) Washfastness can be improved by aftertreating with various substances such as Fixanol (see Appendix, Supply Sources).

TABLE 15

Dye Classes Used with Cellulose Fibers*

	FIBER-REACTIVE DYES	VAT DYES	AZOIC DYES (NAPHTHOL)	DIRECT DYES	ALL-PURPOSE (HOUSEHOLD)
Washfastness	Very good	Excellent	Excellent	Poor-fair	Poor-moderate
Lightfastness	Very good	Excellent	Very good	Good-excellent	Good
Brightness of Colors	Very bright	Muted	Very bright	Muted	Muted
Brand Name Examples	Procion Cibacron	Cibanone	Brentamine Fast Color Salts and Brenthol Coupling Agents	Chlorantine	Putnam Cushing Deka Rit
Comments	Unfixed dye is difficult to remove.	Time-consuming process requiring a skillful dyer.	Limited color range with many bright reds. Difficult to work with.	Easy to use. Better light-fastness than with some reactive dyes.	Expensive way to dye. Dyes are a combination of acid (protein) and direct (cellulose) dyes. The acid portion of the dye is wasted.

*Silk, a protein fiber, can also be dyed with the fiber-reactive and vat dyes.

5. Color

Color has been important to man since he first stood up on his hind legs and moved into a cave. Even then there was a need to decorate the cold dark walls of the cave with mineral and vegetable pigments. Throughout history, as color has been used in many ways to enrich the life of man, the dyer's contribution of colored fiber and cloth has played a significant role.

Originally all colors were produced from natural substances, so the colors of the dyer were limited to what nature had to offer. Though many beautiful subtle shades such as gold, rust, moss green and burnt orange were possible, only a limited number of bright colors could be produced. Today's dyer, however, has access to a large number of synthetic dyes. With these dyes the color range has been expanded to include every conceivable shade.

Color is the dyer's business. By taking advantage of the dyes available today it is possible to mix practically any color by blending the dyes in various percentages. First, however, it is important to understand how color is created and the effect that one color has on another when the units are combined. Only by understanding the nature of color can the dyer creatively manipulate it in the dyepot.

Color Vocabulary

When describing a color, terms such as "dull," "bright," "light" or "dark" are commonly used to explain the physical properties. These terms, however, do not always mean the same thing to each person. The following vocabulary will provide a common ground for discussing the dimensions of color.

HUE: the name of the color such as red, green or blue. Every color falls into a particular hue category as indicated by the names of the colors of the spectrum.

INTENSITY, CHROMA OR SATURATION: the brightness of a color. A color of a fully saturated hue is more intense than a dull color of the same hue—red versus maroon, for instance. A color is made less intense by the addition of its *complement* (see below) or by adding gray, black or white.

VALUE: the lightness or darkness of a color when compared with black or white. Different hues of the same value—bright yellow and light violet, for example—will appear the same shade of gray in a black and white photo. The closer a color is to white, the higher its value; the closer to black, the lower its value. For example, yellow, a light color, has a higher value than violet, a dark color.

TINT: hue + white. In dyeing, this is accomplished by using less dye in the dyepot. Pink is a tint of red.

SHADE: hue + black. In dyeing, a color can also be darkened by adding its complement. Complements produce colors that are more "alive" than if black were used. Burgundy is a shade of red.

TONE: hue + gray. With dyeing this can also be achieved by adding some of the color's complement to the tint of the color. Rosebeige is a tone of red.

COMPLEMENT: the color exactly opposite another on the color wheel; for example, green is the complement of red. Mixing a hue with an equal amount of its complement theoretically yields gray or black, while mixing a hue with a small amount of its complement results in a loss of intensity because of the graying effect.

Tints, shades and tones of a hue result in distinct changes in the value of the color as well as reducing its intensity. In some cases the hue itself is affected. By varying the three dimensions of color (hue, value and intensity) the dyer can mix any color desired.

Color and Light

Color begins with light. This was demonstrated by a famous experiment of Sir Isaac Newton: when he passed a narrow beam of sunlight through a glass prism to break up light into its various component colors, they formed a rainbow-like band that could be seen by the eye. This band is called a color spectrum. It comprises six main divisions of color—red, orange, yellow, green, blue and violet—although the color movement from one

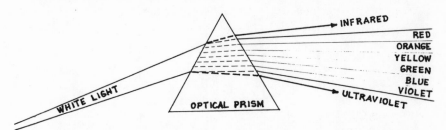

9. A narrow beam of white light passed through a prism of transparent material will spread and separate wavelengths into distinct, identifiable bands of color known as a color spectrum.

band to another is so gradual that the change is imperceptible.

Light is actually electromagnetic energy, which is but one kind of energy known today (some others are thermal, chemical, kinetic, atomic and electrical). In this very broad spectrum of electromagnetic energy, light occupies but one narrow band, located between cosmic rays at one end and electrical power waves at the other. The individual types of electromagnetic energy that compose the spectrum are identified by their wavelengths or frequency ranges.

Light is unique in that it is the only form of electromagnetic energy capable of stimulating the light receptors in the eye which permit color to be seen. For this reason light is often called "visible energy," although the energy itself cannot be seen. The band referred to as light occupies the narrow portion of the spectrum between 380 and 760 millimicrons (mμ). The color violet corresponds to the lower portion of this wavelength band and the color red is located at the upper end. Wavelengths shorter or longer than these are not capable of stimulating the eye, which is why only black is seen for all other forms of electromagnetic energy.

How Color Is Seen

Many people associate color with a physical object, such as a red rose or a copper bowl. Color, however, is not a physical part of

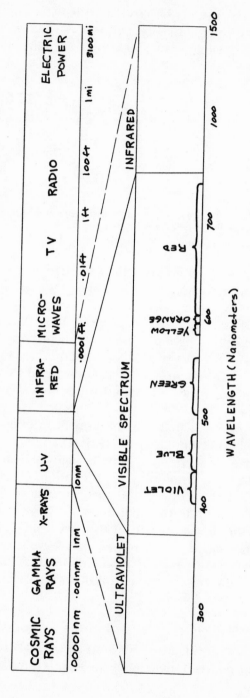

10. Types of electromagnetic energy, of which visible light is but one narrow band (enlarged on the bottom).

what is seen but, as explained above, is the result of the visual sensations produced in the eye by light energy of particular wavelengths. By a process still not completely understood, the eye and the brain supply the idea of color by converting light waves into nervous energy, which results in impulses to the brain producing the idea of color. For example, the longest visible light waves produce a sensation in the brain which is interpreted as "red," while the shortest visible waves are seen as "violet."

The color that is seen is affected by two things: the particular source of light which illuminates the object and the light waves which are absorbed by the coloring agent (for example, dye) in

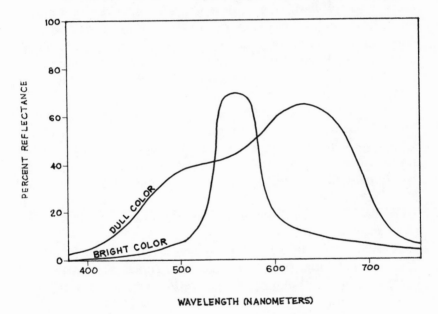

WAVELENGTH (NANOMETERS)

11. Reflectance patterns of a bright dye and a dull dye.

the object. Actually, it is the molecular makeup of the coloring agent that determines how it will respond to a light source. With a dye, the molecular composition of the chromophore determines which light waves are absorbed; every dye is capable of selectively absorbing certain ones. If, for example, the chromophore absorbs all light waves but those producing red, these light waves are reflected back to the eye and the color red is seen.

With certain instruments it is possible to measure which wavelengths are absorbed or reflected and then graphically plot the results. The shape of the curve that is produced indicates the purity of the dye. If light is reflected over a narrow wavelength band (forming a sharp peak) a bright color is seen, while if light is reflected over a broad wavelength band (producing a wide flat curve) then a dull color is seen.

Effect of Light on Color

Color cannot exist without light. The particular light source also influences how the color is seen. Sunlight is the most common source of light. Even colors viewed under daylight conditions, however, will vary depending on the time of day, weather conditions, and geographical location. The same green will appear slightly different when viewed at the North Pole and at the equator, because the composition of the light waves reaching the earth is different at each of these places.

Colors viewed under artificial light will also vary according to the composition of the light source. While some artificial lights emit approximately the same wavelengths as sunlight, other sources vary considerably. Mercury-vapor lamps, for example, are almost totally devoid of red energy. An object that appears red in daylight conditions will be seen as brown under a mercury-vapor light because there is no red light energy available to be reflected back to the eye.

Therefore, it is important for the dyer to consider the source of light when making color decisions. Colors chosen in the evening using artificial light may appear quite different the next morning when the sun is shining. Consider the ultimate use of the fiber when selecting colors. If it is to be used in a tapestry that will be illuminated with a particular light source, choose the colors using the same source. On the other hand, if the fiber is to be used to weave a poncho that will mainly be worn outside during daylight hours, the color decisions should be made in sunlight.

Color Mixing Theories

Every color that is seen is actually the result of a mixture of light waves rather than just one particular wavelength. The number of possible combinations is almost incalculable, which explains why there are so many colors. The mixing of the light waves occurs primarily in two ways, addition or subtraction, and the type of mixing determines the color that is produced. Additive mixtures occur with the mixing or blending of colored lights, while subtractive mixtures result when colored materials such as dyes or pigments are combined.

If we first examine the phenomenon of color production by the addition of light energy, it will be easier to understand how color is obtained subtractively with dyes and pigments.

Additive Color Mixing

Even before color vision was understood, it had been demonstrated that most colors, including white, could be produced by

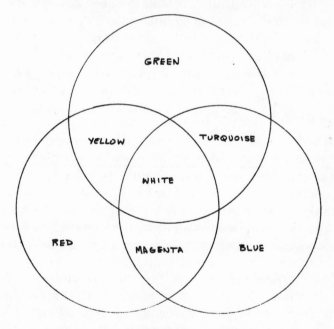

12. Primary and secondary colors of light.

mixing red, green and blue lights. This discovery formed the basis for the additive theory of color, using the colors red, green and blue as *additive primaries*. Any combination of these colors creates additional light energy so that a mixed color is always lighter than the primary colors. When blue and green lights are mixed in equal amounts cyan, a kind of turquoise, appears. This color is lighter than either of its two parent colors because of the increase in light energy. The combination of red plus blue lights produces the color magenta—again, a lighter color than its two parent colors. A more startling effect occurs when red and green are mixed in equal amounts: yellow, a color of obvious lightness, results. And when all three primary colors are combined in equal amounts, white, the lightest of all colors, is created. This explains why daylight, which is composed of all the visible light rays, is seen as "white light."

In each of the combinations discussed above, light has combined with light to give greater light or more energy, resulting in a lighter color being seen. Additive mixing occurs when two or more reflected or transmitted colors are seen as a single color—for example, in the physical blending of colored theatrical lights or the visual blending of colors seen at a distance. Two different colors of yarns in a fabric blend into a third color when the eye sees them at a distance, and tiny colored dots on a color TV screen appear as colored images when mixed by the eye.

Subtractive Color Mixing

With subtractive color mixing, on the other hand, light energy is absorbed or subtracted each time one color is added to another. Because less light energy is available to be reflected back to the eye, a darker color is seen. The colors that are produced by mixing the additive primaries in equal amounts—magenta, turquoise and yellow—are the *subtractive primaries*. Equal amounts of magenta and turquoise produce blue; magenta and yellow give red; and yellow and turquoise combine to yield green. Thus, equal two color blends of the subtractive primaries produce the additive primaries. An equal mixture of all three subtractive primaries results in no color, or black, since all light energy is absorbed. Less-than-equal blends of the three subtractive primaries are used to produce all the other pigment colors.

It can be seen that the effects obtained by mixing dyes or pigments are different from those obtained by mixing colored lights. For example, the mixing of red and green lights produces yellow, and the combination of yellow and blue lights gives white. When red and green pigments are mixed together, however, a dull brown is created, while a blend of yellow and blue dyes yields a green color. In each case the subtractive mixed color is darker

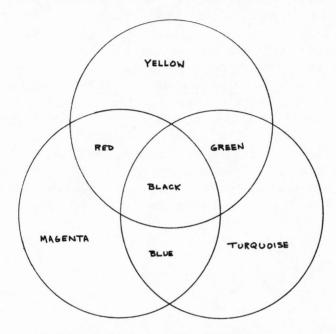

13. Primary and secondary colors of dyes and pigments.

than its two parent colors, while the additive mixed color is always lighter than the parents from which it was blended.

A dye molecule is formulated to absorb all of the colors of the spectrum (violet, blue, green, yellow, orange and red) except the color that gives the dye the name applied to it. Thus, a fabric dyed green absorbs to varying degrees violet, blue, yellow, orange and red, and reflects only green light back to the eye, which is why the fabric appears green. A fabric dyed red absorbs all the spectrum colors but red. When red and green dyes are combined, the red dye absorbs most of the green light and the green dye absorbs most of the red light, so that a very dull color—brown—is seen.

Primary Colors

A *primary color* is one that cannot be mixed using any combination of colors yet that, when mixed with the other primaries, produces almost all the other colors. (Recent chemical advances have produced certain colors, such as shocking pink, which cannot be duplicated through mixing.) Different colors are designated "primaries" in different fields of color study; the physicist works with a different set of primaries than do the artist and the dyer.

As previously stated, the primary colors of the artist and dyer are the subtractive primaries magenta, yellow and cyan. More often, however, the color red is substituted for magenta and the color blue for cyan. This change alters color mixing results. Actually, both reds and both blues are useful as primaries to the dyer because they provide a means of producing a broader color range. Magenta, for example, when mixed with turquoise (cyan) produces a range of intense violets not obtainable with red and blue; turquoise, when mixed with yellow, produces a brighter range of greens than can be obtained using blue. Only by using five primaries (two reds, two blues and one yellow) instead of three is it possible to mix a wide range of intense colors.

Secondary Colors

This term, used mainly by the person working with pigments or dyes, designates the colors that are produced by mixing equal amounts of two primary colors. The intensity of the secondary color depends on which primaries are combined. For example, turquoise plus yellow gives a more intense green than blue plus yellow.

$$
\begin{matrix}
\text{Red + yellow} \\
\text{or} \\
\text{Magenta + yellow}
\end{matrix}
\quad = \text{orange};
$$

$$
\begin{matrix}
\text{Red + blue} \\
\text{or} \\
\text{Turquoise (cyan) + magenta}
\end{matrix}
\quad = \text{violet};
$$

$$
\begin{matrix}
\text{Blue + yellow} \\
\text{or} \\
\text{Turquoise + yellow}
\end{matrix}
\quad = \text{green}
$$

Less-than-equal blends of the primaries, or a mixture of a primary and an adjacent secondary color, are used to produce all the other intense hues. These are referred to as the *intermediate secondary colors*, more commonly called the *intermediate colors*.

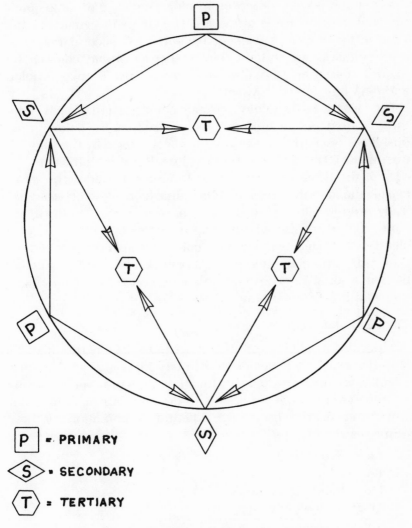

P = PRIMARY

S = SECONDARY

T = TERTIARY

14. Primary, secondary, and tertiary color relationships.

When mixing an intermediate color, consider the effect that one color has on another and base the amount of dye used on the modification that is needed.

Tertiary Colors

The term *tertiary color,* which also applies mainly to the work of the dyer and painter, describes a color composed of some quantity of each of the three primaries. The colors designated as the *major tertiaries* consist of an equal blend of two secondaries. (The three primaries are contained in any two secondary colors.) The major tertiaries are olive (orange + green), rust (orange + violet) and navy blue (green + violet).

Because the tertiary colors contain some portion of each of the three primary colors, they are less intense than the colors previously discussed, due to the graying effect caused by the subtractive mixture. The degree of intensity loss depends on the percentages of the three primaries used to create a shade. The more closely the mixture approaches an equal blend—which theoretically produces black—the less intense the color. On the other hand, the nearer the mixture approximates that of a two-color blend, the greater its intensity. A color whose formula is 30 percent red, 40 percent yellow and 30 percent blue is less intense than another color whose formula is 10 percent red, 70 percent yellow and 20 percent blue.

The Color Wheel

The color wheel is used to demonstrate visually the relationship that exists between three primary hues and all the other colors that can be produced by their mixing. If the dyer is working with five primaries, it is possible to develop four different color wheels, each composed of a different combination of three primaries:

    Red, yellow, blue
    Red, yellow, turquoise
    Magenta, yellow, blue
    Magenta, yellow, turquoise

Although certain color areas are repeated on more than one wheel (the magenta-to-yellow area on wheels three and four or the turquoise-to-yellow area on wheels two and four) there are sections on each wheel that contain hues that are found on none of the others. With four color wheels the dyer can mix a broader range of intermediate and tertiary colors.

The position of a mixed color on the wheel indicates both its parentage and its intensity. The range of shades that can be produced by mixing any two or more colors in various percentages can also be determined from the color wheel. The parentage of a mixed color is indicated by its position in relation to the

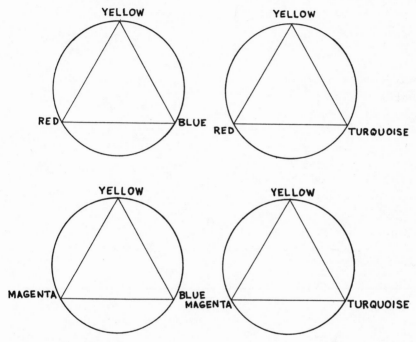

15. With five primaries—red, magenta, yellow, blue, and turquoise—it is possible to construct four different color wheels.

colors from which it was created. If, for example, 50 percent red plus 50 percent yellow were combined, the mixed color would be located halfway between its two parent colors on the color wheel.

The intensity of a color is also shown by its position on the wheel. The more intense primary, secondary and intermediate colors are located on the outer rim of the wheel and the duller tertiary colors are inside. The range of shades that can be produced by mixing two colors in various percentages is demonstrated by connecting these colors with a straight line. Any shade located on this line can be formed from the two colors located on either end.

Color Orientation

The relationship between the mixed colors and the primary hues from which they are created exists because of the way the color wheel is oriented. An understanding of this system is help-

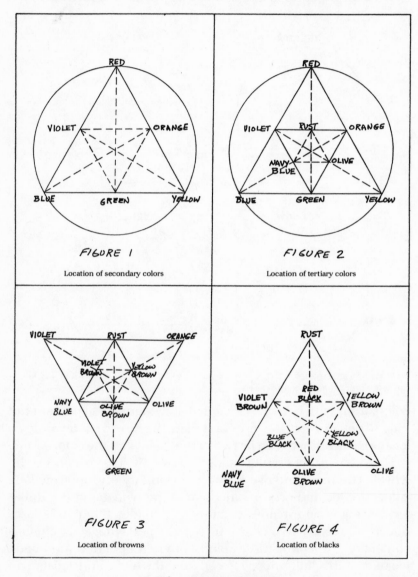

16. Color orientation diagram.

ful to the dyer who wishes to develop a systematic approach to color mixing. A series of triangles formed inside the wheel can be used to illustrate how this system is developed and to show the relationships between the mixed colors.

First, the three primary colors are placed equidistant around the circle by drawing an equilateral triangle inside and letting points indicate their location. The placement of the secondary colors—orange, green and violet—is then determined by extending a straight line from the corner of each triangle to the opposite side of the circle. These secondary points, which represent 50:50 blends of two primaries, also form an equilateral triangle when joined together. The intermediate colors can then be placed along the sides of the triangle between the primary and secondary colors from which they were mixed, with their positions indicating the percentage composition of their two parent colors. All colors located on the sides of the solid-line triangle in figure 1, opposite, are of full intensity.

Because the tertiary colors are less intense than the colors discussed so far, they are located inside the triangle, with their positions indicating the percentage composition of the three primaries from which they were mixed. Their positions also reflect the degree of intensity loss; they decrease in intensity as they move to the triangle's center, which represents black.

The three major tertiary colors are located by drawing straight lines from the angles of the triangle formed by connecting the secondary hues. The points where these dotted lines cross the opposite sides of the interior solid-line triangle locate the major tertiary colors (figure 2):

Orange + green	=	olive
Orange + violet	=	rust
Green + violet	=	navy blue

The three major tertiary colors are then joined to produce a fourth triangle, from which it is possible to locate the positions for the three major browns (figure 3):

Rust + navy blue	=	violet-brown
Rust + olive	=	dark yellow-brown
Olive + navy blue	=	olive-brown or drab

When analyzing a particular brown for the purpose of mixing it is often difficult to determine which colors were blended to obtain that shade. Being aware of some of the browns found in each group helps when mixing similar shades. These include:

> *Yellow Browns:* ivory, blondes, golds, maple, light oaks, tans, amethyst, amber
>
> *Red Browns:* chocolate, mahoganies, oxblood, iron oxide, auburn, henna
>
> *Green Browns:* walnuts, weathered oaks, olive drab, dates, seals, brunettes

A final triangle is formed by connecting the three major browns (figure 4, page 76) with a straight line from which it is possible to locate the blacks including:

Violet-brown + dark yellow-brown = red-black
Violet-brown + drab = blue-black
Dark yellow-brown + drab = yellow-black

Intensity of the Dyes

The intensity of the colors on the triangle discussed above reflects a system based on theoretical color mixes, with all colors on the outside of equal intensity. When working with dyes, however, the system is somewhat altered. This is because the dyes used as the primaries do not exhibit the same spectral properties or the same degree of purity as the primaries used to develop the color wheel. As a result, there is a loss of intensity each time two dyes are mixed. Only those colors produced directly from one dye are of full intensity. With every mixed color there is a graying effect regardless of whether all three primaries are involved.

The spectral properties of a color refer to the amount of light that is absorbed at a particular wavelength. The theoretical primaries on which the color wheel is based are pure colors; they absorb all wavelengths except those of the particular primary color. With dyes, it is not possible to produce a chromophore that absorbs all but one wavelength. Instead, a mixture of wavelengths other than those producing the primary color is reflected back to the eye, slightly reducing the intensity of the color that is seen.

When working with the dyes the color wheel must be adapted to express the intensity loss that occurs whenever the dyes are mixed. Those colors produced directly from the dyes are located on the outer edge of the circle; all the mixed colors, including the mixed secondaries, are placed inside, their position reflecting their lower intensity. Only if the secondary colors are produced

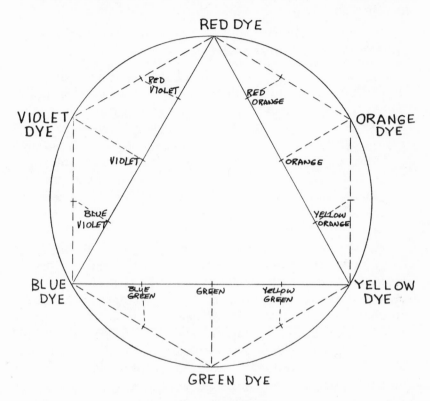

17. Color intensity diagram.

from dyes can they be placed on the outer edge of the circle to show that they are of the same intensity as the primaries.

The position of the intermediate hues is dependent on whether both parent colors were dyes or one was a mixed secondary color. The latter hues will be of lower intensity and will reflect this by a position closer to the center of the circle. The intensity of the tertiary colors also depends on whether they are produced from previously mixed colors or directly mixed from the dyes.

A secondary-primary dye blend will produce more intense

shades than the combination of three primary dyes. The choice of which to use depends on the results desired, but it is important for the dyer to be aware of the variations in intensity that can occur. For practical reasons it is easier to stock and work with only the primary dyes.

Predicting Color Mixing Results

As explained earlier, the color wheel plays an important role in indicating color mixing results because of the relationship that exists between the mixed colors and the three primary hues. The Grumbacher "Color Compass," available at most art stores, is an example of a color wheel which can be used as a visual reference for planning color mixes. By referring to the "Color Identification Chart" contained in the "Color Compass," the dyer can estimate the composition of a color by noting its location on the wheel and visually determine the color range that can be produced by mixing any two or more colors.

A straight line drawn between any two colors on the wheel passes through the range of shades which can be produced from the pair. For example, all the shades which lie on the line connecting red and green can be obtained by mixing these two colors in various proportions. Any point where two or more lines intersect indicates a color that can be mixed using the various parent colors. For example, the lines connecting red-orange with blue-violet, yellow with red-violet, and red with blue-green all pass through point "A." Each of these pairs of colors mixed in the right amounts will yield this color (Diagram 18A).

Lines crossing the circle tend to converge in the center area of browns and blacks, illustrating that the closer the location of a shade to the center, the greater the number of pairs of colors which can be mixed to produce it. This also means that any complementary or near-complementary pair can be used for mixing the browns and blacks. On the other hand, lines connecting colors which pass to either side of the center area demonstrate that there is no way a brown can be mixed using these two colors in any combination. Yellow plus red-violet can produce yellow-brown but there is no way a brown can be obtained by mixing orange plus red-violet (Diagram 18B).

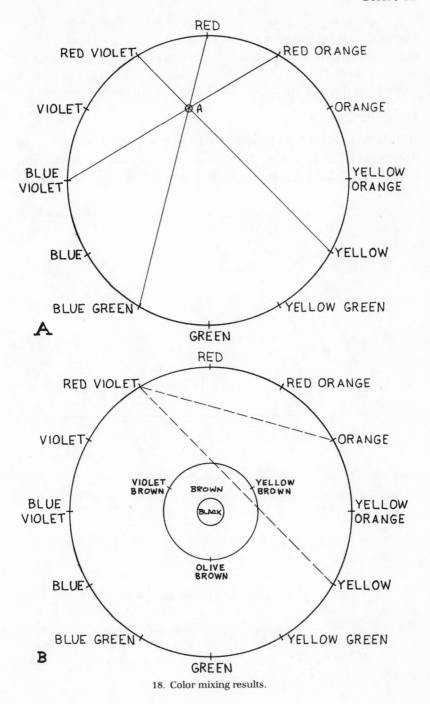

18. Color mixing results.

For the dyer, this means that it is sometimes possible to substitute one pair of colors for another when mixing a color. This is important when, for example, a particular dye is unavailable or not colorfast. By having more than one option available when mixing a color, the dyer can obtain more satisfactory results.

Color Mixing

It was stated at the beginning of this chapter that the main business of the dyer is color. We can now see that "color" should be amended to "color mixing," since this is how the dyer creates color.

The first step when planning a color mix is to analyze the color to determine its three dimensions: hue, intensity and value. Then,

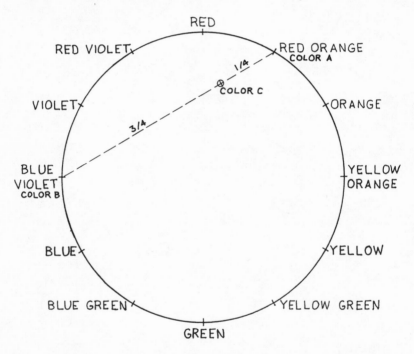

19. The color wheel can be used to formulate theoretical color mixes.

by matching the color to be dyed with a similar color on the wheel, we can determine which colors to mix and how much of each to use.

This is possible because, as previously demonstrated, the position of a color on the wheel indicates the theoretical amounts of each color that are used to produce it. For example, if color A and color B are to be mixed to produce color C, and color C is located one-fourth of the distance from A along the straight line, then it would require three times as much of color A as color B to produce color C (Diagram 19). In other words, the amount of each dye is inversely proportional to the ratio of the distance of each parent color from the mixed shade.

Once the theoretical percentages of each color have been determined, it is necessary to experiment with various trial blends until the desired color is matched. A set of color samples whose formulas are already known will reduce the amount of experimenting that is necessary. (Chapter 9, Gradations, discusses various color mixing systems for obtaining these samples.) While the wheel can be used as a theoretical starting point, the color samples are the foundation for determining actual color mixes since they prove how dyes behave when mixed together. The wheel only indicates how they should behave and, although a valuable tool, it is no substitute for the color samples.

6. The Metric System and the Dyer

Why Use the Metric System?

Just as a beginning weaver must become familiar with the language and methods used in drafting, a beginning dyer must learn language and methods based on scientific techniques. The advantages of the synthetic dyes—which include the ability to mix any color desired with results that can be duplicated—can only be realized if the dyer adopts a system that allows precise measurement of weight and volume. This is why the metric system is used. It provides a method for making accurate measurements in a convenient way, something that is not possible with the U.S. system.

For years now, most countries of the world have been using the metric system. The United States is one of the few exceptions that still follows the more cumbersome and less accurate U.S. systems of feet (length), pounds (weight), gallons (volume) and Fahrenheit (temperature). Scientists in this country, however, have always worked with the metric system. As a dyer, it is time for you to join the scientists and the rest of the world and adopt the metric system.

Common Metric Units and Prefixes

The metric system was invented—it did not evolve—and was based on the latest scientific principles of its time, the late 1700s. The common metric units include the meter (length), gram (weight), liter (volume) and degree centigrade (temperature). Unlike the U.S. units, though, all the metric units have the same prefixes for designating multiples or fractions of the standard units. The prefixes are based on units of ten, the decimal system, which means all that is necessary when increasing or decreasing a measurement is to move the decimal to the right or left. For

TABLE 16

METRIC UNITS

MEASUREMENT	UNIT
Weight	gram
Volume	liter
Temperature	centigrade

example, a milligram is one-thousandth of a gram (1/1,000 or 0.001). The decimal point has been moved three places to the left. The kilogram is 1,000 grams. In this case, the decimal has been moved three places to the right. This is the basis for the entire

TABLE 17

METRIC PREFIXES

PREFIX	MEANING
Centi-	one-hundredth (0.01)
Milli-	one-thousandth (0.001)
Kilo-	a thousand times (1000)

metric system. By learning the few key terms used for units of measurement plus the metric prefixes for designating the amounts of each unit, one can master the system.

Tables 16 and 17 list the common metric units used by the dyer and the prefixes used with them. It is important to realize that there are many other metric prefixes, each designating a tenfold increase or decrease. For the purposes of the dyer, however, the above prefixes are all that are needed. Each of the prefixes can be used with any of the units to designate amounts. "Milliliter," a combination of the prefix "milli-" (one-thousandth) plus the unit "liter," indicates a quantity that is one-thousandth of a liter. It is easier to say "thirty milliliters" than to say "thirty one-thousandths of a liter." "Kilogram" is a combination of the prefix "kilo-" (1,000) and the unit "gram," and indicates an amount of 1,000 grams. Again, it is easier to express a larger amount as "two point three five (2.35) kilograms" than as "two thousand, three hundred and fifty (2,350) grams," although either is correct.

Metric Abbreviations

Because it is time-consuming to write out a unit of measurement each time it is mentioned, a system of abbreviations is used. This is an easy system to learn, since each abbreviation or symbol

TABLE 18

METRIC ABBREVIATIONS

PREFIX	SYMBOL
Kilo-	k
Centi-	c
Milli-	m
UNIT	SYMBOL
Gram	g
Liter	l
Centigrade	C

is the first letter of the prefix or unit which it represents. Table 18 lists those units most commonly needed by the dyer.

Since both "centi-" and "centigrade" start with the letter "c," the abbreviation for "centigrade" is capitalized to show the difference. Using this system, the abbreviation for milliliter is *ml* and the abbreviation for kilogram is *kg*.

The Accuracy of Measurements

The measuring system itself is not what determines the quality of work that can be done. It is the equipment used for performing the measurements that controls this accuracy. Regardless of the skills of the dyer, the degree of accuracy is only as good as the equipment allows. Since the metric system is also the system of science, precision-manufactured instruments and equipment are available which make it possible to obtain accurate measurements. This is where the U.S. system falls short. It was not intended to be used for scientific work. Teaspoons, tablespoons and cups, for example, were never meant to be used for making volume measurements that could be closely reproduced. A much larger percentage error in volume capacity is acceptable in their manufacturing. In addition, this equipment is not intended for making fractional measurements or for dispensing amounts smaller than a quarter of a teaspoon. Such quantities must be

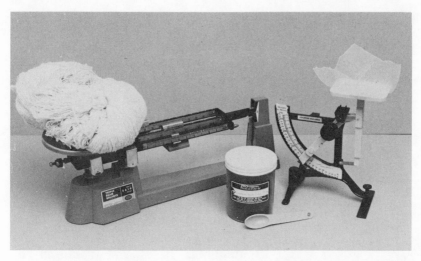

A gram scale is needed for weighing dyes, chemicals and fibers. The inexpensive scale on the right (see Supply Sources) works well for weighing dyes and chemicals. The triple-beam balance (see Supply Sources) can be used for all weighing operations.

estimated. For the dyer who wants color matching, this is not good enough. The more accurate measuring equipment of the scientist must be used.

Measurement of Weight

Most weighing operations done by the dyer concern the weight of the fiber to be dyed, the weight of the dyes used to prepare dyestock solutions and the various chemicals used in the dyeing procedure. Such measurements are made in gram amounts.

The accuracy of any scale is usually directly related to the price. For the purposes of the dyer, an inexpensive and, therefore, less precise metric scale is adequate, but it is important to be consistent with weighing techniques. Many of the less expensive scales now available indicate weights in both the metric and the U.S. systems, which allow the dyer to see the equivalencies between the two systems. The expensive, more accurate scales are reserved for scientific work where very small amounts (milligrams, for example) are measured.

Volume Measurements

It is with volume measurements that the dyer most clearly realizes the advantages of the metric system. This is because many dyeing situations involve the need to measure much smaller amounts than can accurately be dispensed using the equipment of the U.S. system (for example, less than a quarter of a teaspoon). By using the metric measuring devices of the scientist, however, the dyer can measure any liquid amount precisely.

The pipette is the tool of the scientist for measuring small volume amounts. It is manufactured in various sizes and for different purposes but, for the needs of the dyer, a one-ml and a ten-ml "to deliver" pipette are adequate. These pipettes are marked at specific intervals so they can be used for measuring fractional amounts or for dispensing several samples from one filling. The one-ml pipette is graduated in 0.01-ml markings, while the ten-ml pipette is graduated in 0.1-ml amounts and is suited for volumes greater than one ml. When measuring liquid amounts larger than ten mls, the dyer can refill the pipette the necessary number of times. If the volume of liquid is too great to be conveniently measured with a pipette, a larger container, such as the graduated cylinder, is used. Choose the equipment that most closely approximates the volume being measured.

10-ml pipette calibrated in 0.1 ml

1-ml pipette calibrated in 0.01 ml

The graduated cylinder is used for making larger volume measurements that do not have to be as precise. The total volume amount is quite accurate, but intermediate points are less reliable, with measurements in the lower portion giving increasingly larger percentage errors. The size of the measuring container should correlate with the total volume to be measured. Do not, for

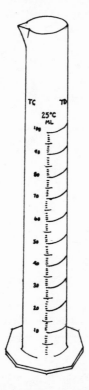

20. A graduated cylinder.

example, choose a 100-ml cylinder to measure fifteen mls; instead, use the ten-ml pipette, filling it one and a half times. Graduated cylinders in both a 100-ml and a 250-ml size are useful sizes for the dyer to have.

Volume measurements for the dyer mainly concern the quantity of dyestock solution used for mixing colors and the amount of water needed in the dyebath. Dyestock solutions often involve small volume amounts, expressed metrically as milliliters, which are measured with the pipette. The amount of water used in the dyebath is usually measured in milliliters or liters. Water can be measured using a graduated cylinder or a large measuring cup with metric markings.

Mathematical Calculations and the Metric System

Mathematical calculations, too, are easier to perform with the metric system than with the U.S. system. This is because there is no need for finding the least common denominator, reducing improper fractions, adding mixed numbers or reducing mixed units to a common base. The following example comparing the two systems to determine the volume of dyestock solution used for a given weight of fiber illustrates this point.

U.S. SYSTEM

Weight of fiber: 1 pound, 5 ounces

Volume of dyestock solution: 2-1/2 teaspoons per ounce of fiber

Method: reduce the fiber weight in pounds and ounces to a common base (21 ounces). Multiply this by the number of teaspoons per ounce:

$21 \times 2\text{-}1/2 = 52\text{-}1/2$ teaspoons dyestock solution

Convert the 52-1/2 teaspoons to cups + teaspoons (there are 48 teaspoons to a cup):

$$\frac{52.5}{48} = 1 \text{ cup} + 4.5 \text{ teaspoons}$$

METRIC SYSTEM

Weight of fiber: 594 grams (1 pound, 5 ounces)

Volume of dyestock solution: 0.5 mls/g of fiber (2-1/2 tsp/oz)

Method: multipy the fiber weight times the number of mls per gram of fiber

$594 \times 0.5 = 297$ mls of dyestock solution

This volume can be measured directly using a graduated cylinder without having to make any conversions.

By now, the dyer should be convinced that the advantages inherent in the metric system far outweigh the inconvenience of learning it. As the preceding problem demonstrates, only with the metric system can volume amounts be measured in a convenient and accurate way.

Learning the Metric System

It is not necessary when making a metric measurement, such as 37 mls or 58 g, to fully understand how this amount would be expressed in ounces or pounds. Learning to "think in metric," like

TABLE 19

METRIC AND U.S. SYSTEMS EQUIVALENTS

METRIC SYSTEM	U.S. SYSTEM
454 grams	1 pound
28 grams	1 ounce
946 milliliters	1 quart
237 milliliters	1 cup
15 milliliters	1 tablespoon
5 milliliters	1 teaspoon

learning to think in French or German, will take some time. Until then, all that is necessary is that the dyer be able to measure the amounts and perform the calculations accurately.

Table 19, showing metric and U.S. equivalents, is included to show the relationship between the more common units of measurements. While memorizing the weight and volume equivalents is not necessary, it is helpful to become familiar with the more common ones. A quart occupies about the same volume as a liter, and a pound is roughly equal to 450 grams.

7. Preparations for Dyeing

Before any dyeing is started, it is a good idea to assemble all of the needed equipment and become familiar with its use. While most of the equipment is routinely used in the home and requires no

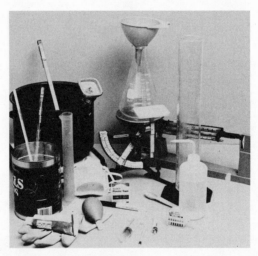

Equipment for dyeing. Note the plastic tape and the laundry pen (center). This equipment works well for labeling fibers before dyeing. ReDuRan (in palm of rubber glove) is a hand cleaning paste specially formulated for removing dyes and inks. Other equipment displayed that may be unfamiliar to the dyer includes the Erlenmyer flask (sitting on scale pan) which can be used for preparing stock solutions, a wash bottle (far right) which is handy for transferring pasted dyes to a larger container, and two sizes of graduated cylinders which are useful for measuring dye and chemical solutions and water when preparing stock solutions.

special knowledge, items such as the pipette and the graduated cylinder are less common and are unfamiliar to most new dyers. Of course it is possible to dye fiber without using these special materials, but the colors obtained cannot be closely matched. It should be the goal of every dyer to be able to control the colors that are produced and not be content with accepting colors that cannot be duplicated. This is only possible by learning to use the tools of the trade.

Once all of the materials needed for dyeing have been gathered, reserve them for this purpose only. The pot now used for dyeing should never double as the spaghetti cooker. Just as any household chemicals are potentially hazardous, dyes are also chemicals which can be harmful if improperly used. To prevent skin rashes or allergic reactions, wear rubber gloves when handling the dyes and avoid breathing the dye powder.

Equipment

STAINLESS STEEL OR ENAMEL POTS: choose a pot that allows for sufficient depth of liquid so that the fiber will be completely immersed. Canning kettles (8-9 liters) are especially handy for 450-gram (1-pound) amounts of fiber and for holding canning jars when dyeing small amounts of fiber.

STIRRING RODS OF GLASS, POLYPROPYLENE OR STAINLESS STEEL: wood will absorb dye material and could contaminate future dyebaths. Glass or polypropylene stirring rods are especially good because they do not stain or transfer dye when going from one pot to another. However, they are not strong enough for lifting wet fibers; here a large stainless steel spoon or rod works well.

THERMOMETER: for measuring the temperature of the dyebath. A candy thermometer with Fahrenheit markings is suitable. It is not necessary to use a centigrade thermometer; its use does not increase the accuracy of the process.

STOCK SOLUTION CONTAINERS: for the acid dyes, containers must be able to withstand boiling water; for the reactive dyes, any suitable size container such as a wine jug may be used. A one-liter size is fine unless you are dyeing in large volumes.

PLASTIC TUBS OR BUCKETS: for scouring, soaking and rinsing yarns.

STAINLESS STEEL OR PLASTIC SPOONS: for handling dye powder when weighing and when mixing stock solutions.

GLASS OR PLASTIC MEASURING CONTAINERS WITH METRIC MARK-INGS: large measuring cups work well for measuring the water used in the dyebath. A 100- or 250-ml graduated cylinder (see Suppliers, page 159) is used for the accurate measuring of large volumes of dyestock solution. The nonbreakable, polypropylene cylinders are recommended.

SCALE OR BALANCE: for weighing dyes, chemicals and fibers. Many dye distributors sell an inexpensive gram scale that works well for weighing dyes and chemicals. For the serious dyer, a triple beam balance (see photo p. 87) is recommended. Always use weighing paper (for example, waxed paper) or a container when measuring dyes and chemicals to prevent contamination of the scale pan.

PIPETTES OR SYRINGES: for accurately measuring small amounts of dyestock solution. Both a one-ml and a ten-ml size are useful. Medicinal syringes, available in various sizes through drugstores and veterinary clinics, can be substituted for the pipette, but they do not measure as accurately. They can be used for dispensing such ingredients as acetic acid (vinegar), which do not require precise measurement.

PIPETTE BULB: used in place of mouth suction to draw the liquid into the pipette. An ear syringe, available at most drugstores, works quite effectively for this purpose. If other types of pipette bulbs are used, they should be loose-fitting so they can easily be removed. The finger is used to control the release of the liquid.

RUBBER GLOVES: to protect the hands when handling dyes, chemicals and hot yarns.

HEAT SOURCE: a kitchen stove or a hot plate. Should have a means for controlling temperature.

SAFETY GOGGLES: worn to protect the eyes from accidental splashing of dyes or chemicals.

FACE MASK OR RESPIRATOR: should always be worn when handling dye powders or toxic chemicals.

pH PAPER: for testing pH of spent dyebaths when adjusting to neutral (pH 7) before disposing.

WASH BOTTLE (Optional): useful for transferring pasted dye powders to a larger container and for dispensing liquids such as the washing soda solution used to neutralize acid dyebaths.

ERLENMEYER FLASK (Optional): useful for preparing dyestock solutions. The flasks are available in many sizes including 100 ml, 500 ml, and 1000 ml size.

Pocket Calculator: simplifies mathematical calculations.

Use of the Pipette

The pipette is filled by suction with the pipette bulb. First, expel all air from the bulb and then place it over the pipette. If using the ear syringe, place the pointed end on the top of the pipette. Draw the dye solution into the pipette, bringing it above the calibration mark closest to the amount to be measured. Then remove the bulb and place the index finger over the top. Through

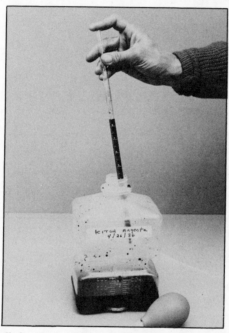

The pipette is controlled with the fleshy portion of the index finger of the dominant hand. To regulate the flow of dye from the pipette, either roll or slightly lift the index finger to break the vacuum. The dye remaining in the pipette tip is included in the calibration and is removed by blowing. Never pipette dyes with the mouth! Instead, use a pipette bulb (displayed in front of stock solution container) which is held in the opposite hand to draw dye solutions into the pipette. Pipettes should be stored upright so they can drain after rinsing.

a motion of release and hold, gradually lower the liquid to the desired mark. Be sure that the index finger is perfectly dry or the pipette will be hard to regulate. Learning to control the pipette is easily accomplished and can be practiced using a glass of water.

After drawing the dye down to the desired line, allow the solution to run into the dyepot. Dye industry pipettes are calibrated with white markings so that the numbers can easily be read when the pipette is filled with colored dye solutions. These pipettes are calibrated to include the volume contained in the tip which should be removed by blowing or expelling with the pipette bulb. Do not rinse the pipette to flush out the solution that remains inside.

Rinse the pipette thoroughly with water immediately after using and place it tip down in a tall container with paper crumpled on the bottom to protect the tip. Pipettes can easily be broken and should be handled carefully.

Use of the Graduated Cylinder

The graduated cylinder is mainly used to measure amounts of dyestock solution or acetic acid too large to be conveniently

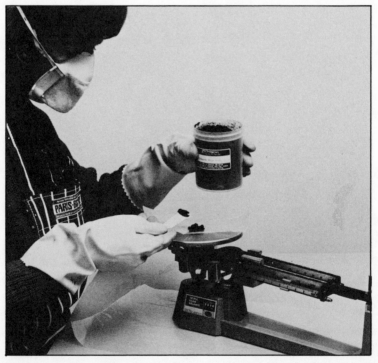

Weighing the dye powder. Note the waxed paper used to prevent contamination of the scale pan. Rinse the paper to remove traces of dye powder before discarding.

handled with a pipette. To use the cylinder, place it on a level surface and fill with liquid until the bottom of the meniscus is on the appropriate mark for the amount being dispensed. (The *meniscus* is the concave surface of the liquid formed when the liquid wets the container wall. It occurs only in glass cylinders and not in polypropylene ones.) All readings should be made at eye level.

Use of the Scale

The main consideration when weighing is that the scale be "zeroed in" prior to use. This must be checked each time the scale is moved.

This process must also include the weighing paper or container, or these may be weighed separately and a proper allowance made for them. Most scales have some type of adjustable weight mounted on screws which can be turned one way or the other to bring the empty reading to zero.

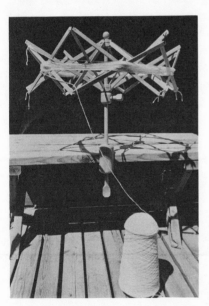

An umbrella swift works well for preparing large skeins of yarn.

When measuring a specified amount, such as a certain quantity of dye powder, use a small, flat-bladed knife or a small spoon for retrieving the material. The dye is easier to handle if it is first placed in a well-labeled container. The powder can then be removed with the knife or spoon and gently tapped into the scale pan until the proper quantity has been deposited. It is important that only clean utensils be used to retrieve the dye powder and that weighing paper or a container be used to prevent contamination of the scale pan. When handling the dye powder, a face mask or respirator and rubber gloves should always be worn. Never weigh dye powders in an area where food is prepared.

Skeining

After gathering the equipment and becoming familiar with its use, it is time to prepare the fiber or fleece that is to be dyed. If working with fiber, form all the yarns into skeins. In this form there is less chance for tangling to occur and the dye solution is able to penetrate the fiber more evenly. All skeins should then be loosely but securely tied with string in several places in a figure-eight fashion to keep them orderly during dyeing. To make it easier to find and discard the ties after dyeing, use cotton string to tie protein fibers and wool yarn to tie cellulose fibers. The ties will come out of the dyebath a different color from the skeins. If dyeing fleece, encase it in a nylon net bag to help protect it from felting. The skeins and/or fleece should then be labeled with waterproof tape and laundry marking pen. This prevents the information from becoming lost when the fiber is immersed in water during the dyeing process.

A convenient method for forming small skeins of yarn. Skeins of similar weight can be prepared by counting the number of wraps around the hand and elbow.

When dyeing fiber samples for determining color formulas it is desirable to work with skeins of the same weight. It is not necessary to weigh each skein, however, if the same yarn is used throughout. Carefully measure several skeins by counting the number of wraps around the thumb and elbow needed to produce a skein of the predetermined weight. Once the count has been determined, it is only necessary to count the wraps for all additional samples. Most plied commercial yarns will produce skeins of the same weight per length because the plying tends to even out any inconsistencies in the spinning process.

22. Several figure-eight ties should be used to loosely secure all skeins
of yarn prior to dyeing.

Scouring

All yarns and fabric should be weighed before scouring, and
the information recorded in a notebook. If the fiber is quite dirty
the dirt could affect the weighing accuracy. In this case, first
scour the fiber, dry it and then record the weight. Generally this
is not necessary; but if you are uncertain, wash a small portion of
the fiber to see if the weight has changed significantly.

Whether you are using handspun yarn, commercially spun
yarn or fabric, it must first be scoured before dyeing. It is necessary to remove as much lanolin and dirt as possible from handspun yarn to ensure even penetration of the dye and avoid streaking. Commercial yarns are scoured to remove sizing, spinning oil
and any other substances that may have been applied at the mill.
Commercial fabrics are washed to remove starch and bleach
residues. Scouring, however, will not remove such finishes as
permanent press or wash-and-wear. Do not attempt to dye
fabrics with those finishes. If the dye solution cannot penetrate
the fiber evenly, those parts reached first will dye darker. This
means an oily or dry spot will receive less dye and a light spot or
streak will result.

Protein fibers can be scoured by soaking in hot water (120° F)
to which a neutral detergent such as Ivory Liquid, Basic H or
Orvus paste has been added. Liquid detergents are preferred because they are easier to rinse out. Handle fibers gently to avoid
felting.

Cellulose fibers, especially cottons, require a special scouring process in preparation for dyeing with reactive dyes to remove all sizing and starch materials which often contain cellulose and will react with the dyes. Scour by boiling the fiber for 30 minutes with a neutral detergent. Synthrapol, a commercial scouring agent, works especially well using ¼-½ teaspoon per gallon of water. Poorer grade cottons may require a second boil. Rinse fiber thoroughly before dyeing.

It is not necessary to dry the fiber if the dye process is to be performed soon. This is why it is important to weigh the yarn or fabric first; otherwise, it would have to be dried, weighed and then rewetted for dyeing.

Washing Fleece

The following recipe works well for scouring fleece. Fleece should be encased in a mesh bag for ease of handling and to minimize fiber damage.

TABLE 20

1. Hot (120° F) water plus soap soak. Orvus paste (available from animal feed supply stores) and liquid dishwashing detergents work well for scouring fleece. Add enough detergent so that the water feels very slippery; avoid making suds. Allow fleece to soak only a short time to avoid allowing the water to cool.
2. Hot water soak. Allow fiber to soak in clean, hot water for a short time. Do not add soap.
3. Hot water plus vinegar rinse. Allow fiber to soak for a short time in hot water to which a little vinegar has been added to cut alkalinity.
4. Hot water rinse, no vinegar. Repeat hot water rinse if traces of soap are evident.

Wetting of Fiber

Even if the yarn, fleece or fabric has been previously cleaned and dried, it must be thoroughly wetted before dyeing. Dry fiber resists the penetration of liquids, causing uneven dyeing. (Of course, this fact may be used to advantage if a variegated effect is desired.) Soak the fiber in warm water for at least twenty minutes before dyeing, then squeeze out the excess water just before placing it in the dyepot.

Kiton acid dyes in stepped increments at .25% intensity, form this color triangle by Judith Hartz. Two primaries are used in each of the edge segments, and all three are used in each interior segment.

Charlotte Elich-McCall has explored Lanaset dyes on wool and silk in many different color progressions in her dye notebook. Good records are essential to repeatable dyeing. PHOTOS: JOE COCA

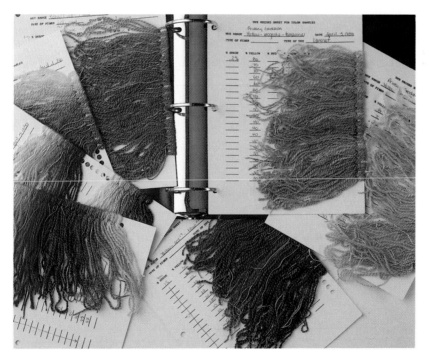

"Spectral Analysis of a Star" (detail) by Laura Militzer Bryant. Wool double weave, yarns dyes with Lanaset and Kiton acid dyes. PHOTO BY PHOTOTEC.

One hundred percent cotton fabric designed and woven for the Arizona Maid of Cotton by Peter Brown. Twenty-five different baths of fiber reactive dye achieve the subtle color progression.   PHOTO: PETER G. BROWN

"Rainbow" batts by Mostly Handspun, a wool processing cooperative. Fleece dyed with 1:2 premetallized (Cibalan) dyes is custom blended during carding. Also shown are yarns spun from various rainbow batts. PHOTO: LINDA KNUTSON

"Libby's Hippari", a three-quarters length coat by Tim Harding. Cotton fabric is dyed with fiber reactive dyes, then quilted, slashed and frayed.

PHOTO: JONETTE NOVAK

"Slide Area" (37" × 36") by Jan Myers. Cotton fabric is dyed with fiber-reactive dyes, then pieced and quilted to give a feeling of space and distance.

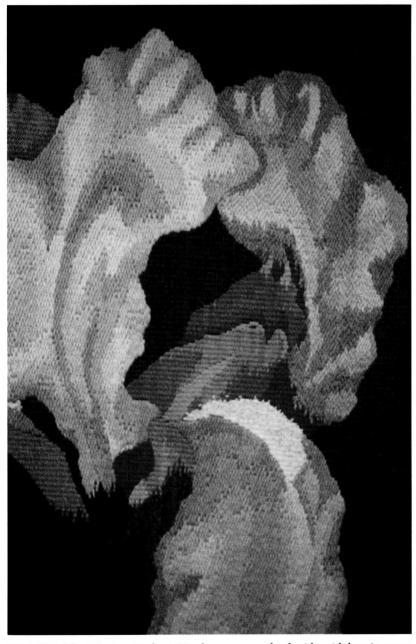

"Iris" (detail) by Winston Herbert. Wool yarns were dyed with acid dyes in many values of each color to create the subtle shading of the flower. PHOTO: BY THE ARTIST

Detail of silk shawls in various weaves by Randall Darwall. The color has been added in some warp sections by dip dyeing, and removed in others by stripping with sodium hydrosulphite. PHOTO: MORGAN ROCKHILL.

8. Dyeing Procedure

Safety and Dyeing

Both environmental and health concerns should be considered when working with dyes and the chemicals associated with their use. In preparation for dyeing, take the time to learn about the dyes and chemicals that are going to be used and become aware of any special precautions or handling techniques that should be observed. Also learn about the proper disposal methods for the materials being used. Some distributors provide safety and disposal information in their catalogs. If this material is not offered, contact the supplier and request this information.

Material safety data sheets are available for every product, including dyes, that are sold to the home dyer and these can be requested from the dealer. These sheets include information on the toxicity of the chemicals, if known, special handling and disposal information and what to do in case of ingestion or spills.

While some dyes contain known carcinogens and some chemicals associated with dyeing are hazardous to work with or dispose of, there are much safer dyes and chemicals available for dyeing. The home dyer does not need to work with any dyes or chemicals that currently pose a health or environmental problem. Purchase dyes and chemicals only from distributors who are knowledgeable about their products and are willing to provide safety information to their customers.

Handling of Dyes and Chemicals

Common sense and good laboratory technique are the keys to safe dyeing. All equipment used for dyeing should be reserved for that purpose only. A pot used for dyeing should not double as the spaghetti cooker for dinner. Never eat, smoke or drink when handling dyes. Always clean up spills; dye solutions become dye powders when dry.

If it is necessary to dye in the kitchen, be sure all food is put away and counter surfaces covered with disposable material such as newspaper. To minimize contamination, never measure dye powders in the kitchen. Also, do not store any dyes, chemicals or stock solutions in the kitchen where they may be confused with foods. These products should be properly labeled and stored in some other area where children do not have access.

When handling dye powders, always wear a dust mask or respirator and gloves. Many dyes can cause lung, skin and eye irritations and some dyes have been known to cause sensitizing reactions. Therefore, avoid any method of dyeing that could cause the formation of dye dust such as the sprinkling of dye powder into the dyepot to create special color effects. Also, use a damp cloth or mop rather than a broom or dust rag when cleaning the work area so that dust is not airborne. And rinse all weighing paper before disposing.

Once dyes are in solution, they are safer to work with. The dyer, however, should take the necessary precautions to minimize contact with dyes and chemicals. Always wear rubber gloves and keep hands out of the dyepot. A plastic apron or smock that can be left in the dye area can be worn to protect clothes. Never mouth pipette any dyes. And work in an area with adequate ventilation—that means a good fan, not an open window—so that fumes are removed from the workspace.

Protective eye glasses should be worn when working with dyes and chemicals, especially acids, as these products can cause eye irritation or burns. If material is splashed into the eye, flush immediately with large amounts of water and contact a doctor.

Disposal of Dyes and Chemicals

The quantity of dye waste generated by the home dyer should not present a disposal problem if handled correctly. Proper handling includes neutralizing any dyebath below a pH of 6 (too acidic) or above a pH of 11 (too alkaline), and flushing all waste material with a large volume of water after pouring down the drain. Also, it is important that the dyeing be properly done to minimize the quantity of waste products produced. This means exhausting all dyebaths as completely as possible and using the amounts of dyes and chemicals recommended in the dyeing procedure (do not just dump).

The pH (acidity or alkalinity) of the dyebath can be determined with pH litmus paper (see Supply Sources). To neutralize an acid dyebath, slowly add a dilute amount of a weak alkali, such as washing soda, until the pH of the dyebath is approximately 7 (neutral). To neutralize a too alkaline bath, add a weak solution of acetic acid.

Under current regulations, dyes that contain heavy metals such as chrome or copper (some premetallized dyes) are strictly regulated but can be discharged into a sewer system in small quantities. There is some possibility of septic tank problems using dyes that contain heavy metals, even though the metals are tightly bound to the dye molecules. The disposal of nonmetallic dyes is not regulated at this time. Regardless of the type of dye being used, however, it is important that the dyebath be exhausted as completely as possible.

Production dyers, who work with much larger volumes of dyes and chemicals, should check with their local environmental agency for information on disposal regulations. The State Department of Ecology can also assist with this information. It is very important that production dyers neutralize acidic dyebaths as too acid a discharge can damage the cement pipes in a sewer system.

The Dyestock Solution

The first step in any dyeing operation is the preparation of *dyestock solutions* for each of the dyes to be used. A dyestock solution is a certain weight of dye powder dissolved in a specific volume of water, for example, one gram of dye powder in 100 mls of water. (A measured amount of stock solution will later be added to a specified volume of water in the dyepot.) The ratio of dye powder to volume of water is expressed as a percentage, and this percentage is the stock solution concentration. For example, one gram of dye powder in 100 mls of water can be written as:

$$\frac{1 \text{ gram dye powder}}{100 \text{ mls water}} = 0.01$$

To convert 0.01 to a percent, multiply by 100:
0.01 × 100 = 1% stock solution

The stock solution is used in place of the direct weighing of the dye powder because it is difficult to measure small quantities of powder accurately. With the inexpensive scales normally used by the dyer, it is not possible to precisely measure less than a gram. But by dissolving one gram of dye powder in 100 mls of water and then measuring one ml of dye solution with a pipette, the dyer can measure 0.01 gram of dye powder in its dissolved state. Only by making measurements in volume quantities rather than in weight amounts can the dyer measure small quantities easily and accurately.

TABLE 22

STORAGE LIFE OF DYESTOCK SOLUTIONS

BRAND	SERIES	SHELF LIFE	STORAGE CONDITIONS
Procion	MX	1-2 weeks	A drop of vinegar to lower the pH of the solution and refrigeration will help to ensure the maximum shelf life.
Procion	H, H-E	4-8 weeks	Same as above.
Cibacron	F	1-3 months	Same as above.
Acid dyes	All series	6 months	Store in a cool, dark place.

The life of a stock solution varies with the class of dye being used. With the reactive dyes it also depends on the dye series.

With the fiber-reactive dyes, the stock solution gradually becomes weaker during storage because of hydrolysis, the chemical process in which the dye reacts with the water and is no longer available to bond with the fiber. As Table 22 illustrates, the reactive dyes of some series hydrolyze more rapidly than others. Elevated temperature and alkaline pH accelerate this process. Since most municipal water is slightly alkaline, adding a drop of vinegar lowers the pH. (This is not necessary if your water is neutral or slightly acid.) Refrigeration also slows down the hydrolyzing reaction.

When dyeings become weaker, it is time to throw out the stock solution and prepare a fresh one. The fiber-reactive stock solutions should be discarded as soon as they show signs of weakening. The acid dyes, however, may be kept for up to six months, at which time they too should be discarded and fresh solutions prepared.

Base the volume of stock solution to prepare on an estimate of how much dyeing will be done within the storage life of the dye. It is both time-consuming and frustrating to have to stop and make up additional quantities of stock solution when it is just as easy to prepare an adequate volume initially. Of course, if large quantities of fiber or fabric are being dyed, this is not possible. Regardless of the type of dye being used, it takes approximately 900 mls, or about one quart of 1 percent stock solution, to dye a pound of fiber a medium shade.

The 1 Percent Stock Solution

A stock solution could conceivably be prepared in any percentage concentration desired. A 1 percent concentration is easiest to work with, however, because it simplifies mathematical calculations: all equations are either multiplied or divided by one. In addition, as the concentration of a stock solution increases it becomes increasingly difficult to accurately measure small amounts of dye.

As previously mentioned, a 1 percent solution means that there is one gram of dye powder in 100 mls of water. One hundred mls is such a small volume (about one-half cup) that, as mentioned above, a larger amount (based on the quantity that can be used within the shelf life of the particular dye) should be prepared.

FORMULA 1: A 1 percent dyestock solution

$$\frac{\text{total volume stock solution}}{100 \text{ mls}} = \begin{array}{l} \text{amount of dye powder for} \\ \text{a 1\% stock solution} \end{array}$$

If, for example, a dyer wants to determine how much dye powder is required to prepare 850 mls of 1 percent dyestock solution, then, according to Formula 1:

$$\frac{850 \text{ mls}}{100 \text{ mls}} = 8.5\text{g of dye powder}$$

If, for some reason, a stock solution other than 1 percent is used, the following formula can be applied to determine the quantity of dye powder:

$$\frac{\text{total volume stock solution}}{100 \text{ mls}} \times \% \text{ stock solution} = \begin{array}{l}\text{grams of}\\\text{dye powder}\end{array}$$

To prepare 850 mls of a 3% dyestock solution:

$$\frac{850 \text{ mls}}{100 \text{ mls}} \times 3 = 25.5\text{g of dye powder}$$

The dyer without accurate weighing equipment can prepare a 1 percent stock solution by dissolving the one-ounce package of dye in three quarts of water. This will give approximately a 1 percent solution.

$$\frac{1 \text{ oz. dye powder}}{3 \text{ quarts water}} = \frac{1 \text{ oz (28g)}}{96 \text{ oz (2838 mls)}} = 0.01 \times 100 = 1\frac{1}{4}\% \text{ stock solution}$$

Preparing the Stock Solution

ACID DYES

After determining the volume of stock solution to be prepared and calculating the grams of dye powder needed, weigh out the dye (see Chapter 7).

Several different methods can be used to dissolve the dye powder. One way is to first paste the powder in a small container such as a plastic cup using a small volume of warm water. Then rinse the dye into a larger container, using several small volumes of hot water to complete the transfer, and add boiling water to bring the dye up to volume. It is important to measure the volume of water accurately using a graduated cylinder or Erlenmyer flask (see photo page 107) or else the stock solution concentration will be affected.

While the above method works well for most acid dyes, some dyes tend to form a tar-like ball which is difficult to dissolve in boiling water, particularly the leveling acid blue dye (Acid Blue 45). An alternative method for dissolving the dye powder is to place boiling water in a stainless steel or glass container using about a third of the total volume needed. Then, while rapidly stirring the water, gradually add the dye powder to the vortex that is formed. Additional boiling water is then added to bring the solution up to volume.

Regardless of how carefully the dye solution has been prepared, a wise precaution is always to check the stock before using to make sure there is no deposit on the bottom. If any powder remains undissolved, the stock solution concentration will be lower than expected, altering dye mixing results. Also, some dyestuffs tend to settle out or curdle. If this happens, place the container in a pan of warm water and gently heat and stir until the dye redissolves. If mold has formed in storage, skim it from the surface or filter the dye solution by pouring it through a double thickness of cheesecloth or pantyhose. Then heat the solution to destroy the spores that remain. It still can be used.

Transferring the pasted dye to a large container. Several small volume rinses work best for removing all traces of the paste. Either a graduated cylinder (shown on left) or an Erlenmyer flask (center) can be used for measuring the water. Some dye distributors sell calibrated beakers (not shown) which also work well.

FIBER-REACTIVE DYES

The fiber-reactive dyes are quite soluble in water. As with the acid dyes, the powder can first be pasted with a small amount of cold water to ensure that it is completely dissolved. Do not add any wetting agents. Then add hot water (about 120° F.) based on the amount needed for the quantity of stock solution being prepared. Stir well to dissolve the paste completely.

An alternative method is to stir the hot water rapidly while carefully adding the dye powder to the vortex. For the reasons mentioned earlier, a drop of vinegar can be added to the stock solution to lower the pH. The solution should then be refrigerated.

Once the dye powder is in solution, it is ready to be used. All stock solutions should be properly labeled with the date prepared, color, dye type and percent strength. When not being used, they should be properly stored out of reach of children or pets. Some solutions look good enough to drink!

Depth of Shade

The first thing the dyer needs to determine is the weight of the fiber being dyed since all dye calculations are based on fiber weight. Then the dyer must calculate how much dye to use to produce the desired color. Perhaps the dyer wants to produce a medium shade of green or a pale tint of blue. Obviously, for a given fiber weight, more dye is required to obtain the darker shade than the lighter tint. The dyer, however, needs to be able to relate these color values to a specific quantity of dye.

This is done by expressing the amount of dye used as a percent of the fiber weight and is referred to as the "Depth of Shade". A 1% Depth of Shade, abbreviated as "DOS", tells the dyer that there is 1 gram of dye per 100 grams of fiber:

$$\frac{1 \text{ gram dye}}{100 \text{ grams fiber}}$$

Two grams of dye for each 100 grams of fiber: is called a 2% DOS.

$$\frac{2 \text{ g dye}}{100 \text{ g fiber}}$$

FORMULA 2

$$\text{Depth of Shade} = \frac{\text{grams of dye}}{100 \text{ grams fiber}}$$

Using the above formula, to determine the grams of dye multiply the DOS by the fiber weight. For example, it would take 1.74 grams of dye to obtain a 3% DOS for 58g fiber.

equation a:

$$\text{weight of dye} = 58 \text{ g fiber} \times \frac{3 \text{ g dye}}{100 \text{ g fiber}} = 1.74 \text{ g dye}$$

Since the home dyer works with dyes in solution, however, it is necessary to convert grams of dye to milliliters (ml) of stock solution. This is done by multiplying by 100 since, by definition, there is one gram of dye for each 100 ml of 1% stock solution.

equation b:

$$\text{volume of 1\% stock} = 1.74 \text{ g dye} \times \frac{100 \text{ ml 1\% stock}}{1 \text{ g dye}} = 174 \text{ ml 1\% stock}$$

Equations "a" and "b" can be combined giving:

equation c:

$$\text{volume of 1\% stock} = 58 \text{ g fiber} \times \frac{3 \text{ g dye}}{100 \text{ g fiber}} \times \frac{100 \text{ ml 1\% stock}}{1 \text{ g dye}} = 174 \text{ ml 1\% stock}$$

Notice in the preceding equation (equation c) how all the units and numbers cancel except for the numbers "58" and "3" and the unit "ml 1% stock". This allows the equation to be simplified and rewritten as:

volume of 1% stock = 58 × 3 = 174 ml

As shown by the above example, to calculate the total volume of 1% stock, multiply the *fiber weight times DOS expressed as a number rather than as a percentage.* For example, it takes 108 ml of 1% stock to dye 216 g of fiber a 0.5% DOS.

volume 1% stock = 216 × 0.5 = 108 ml

It requires 177 ml of 1% stock to dye 115 g of fiber a 1.5% DOS.

volume 1% stock = 115 × 1.5 = 177 ml

FORMULA 3
total volume of 1% stock = fiber weight × DOS (expressed as a number)

Color Value and Depth of Shade

Because a 2% DOS uses twice as much dye as a 1% DOS, the color value of the dyeing is darker. Conversely, a 0.5% DOS, which uses half the dye of a 1% DOS, produces a lighter value. Therefore, the Depth of Shade not only specifies the grams of dye, but also indicates the lightness or darkness of the dyeing. Stated another way, the total volume of stock solution, as calculated using formula 3, determines the color value of the dyeing.

To determine the color value produced by a particular Depth of Shade, dye a value gradation ranging from very pale to deep. In general, Depths of Shade below 0.5% give pale values, 0.5% to 2.0% Depths of Shade appear light-medium to medium, and Depths of Shade above 2.0% to 4.0% are medium-dark to deep. With most dye types, a 4% DOS is as deep a value as can be achieved. Up to a 6% DOS, however, can be used with the fiber reactive dyes to obtain dark values.

TABLE 23

COLOR VALUE EXPRESSED AS DEPTH OF SHADE

COLOR VALUE	DEPTH OF SHADE
Very Pale	0.1%
Pale	0.2%
Light	0.5%
Medium	1.0%
Dark	2.0%
Deep	4.0%

Table 23 gives only an approximation of the color value obtained at a particular Depth of Shade. This is because not all dye series are the same strength. For example, a 1% DOS dyeing with the leveling acid dyes appears a darker value than a 1% DOS produced with the Cibacron F dyes. It takes about a 2% DOS dyeing with the Cibacron F dyes to achieve the same color value as obtained by the 1% DOS leveling acid dyeing. Sampling is the only way to determine the color value and Depth of Shade relationship.

In addition, within a dye series some colors are stronger than others, and at the same Depth of Shade, the stronger dyes will produce a deeper value than the tinctorially weaker dyes. Magenta and turquoise, for example, are stronger than red and blue with the leveling acid dyes.

Percent of Color

Formula 3 is adequate if the dyer is working with just one color. Most colors, however, are produced by mixing two or more dyestock solutions. Therefore, it is necessary to calculate the volume of each dyestock solution that makes up the total volume. Often a formula is available for the color being mixed, with each color expressed as a percent, such as 60% magenta and 40% turquoise. In such cases, the dyer can calculate the volume of the individual color by multiplying the percent of each color by the total volume of the stock solution (formula 3). For example, to dye 120 g of fiber a 2% DOS using the color formula 20% magenta and 80% turquoise, first calculate the total volume of stock solution for a 2% DOS.

total volume 1% stock = 120 × 2 (2% DOS) = 240 ml

Remember: The Depth of Shade (DOS) is expressed as a number rather than as a percent when multiplying because of the way the units and numbers cancel (review formula 3).

Then multiply the % of each color times the total volume:

volume of 1% magenta stock $= 240 \times 0.20^1 = 48$ ml

$+$

volume of 1% turquoise stock $= 240 \times 0.80 = 192$ ml

total volume of stock $= 240$ ml*

(*Always check that the sum of the individual volumes equals the total stock solution volume to ensure calculations are correct. A calculator reduces the chance of error.)

FORMULA 4

volume of 1% stock solution for an individual color = fiber weight × DOS × % of color

Note that formula 4 is actually formula 3 to which "× % of color" has been added.

Some dyers prefer to mix colors instinctively by blending various amounts of dyes. It is still important to note the volume of each color used so that a color formula can be determined and recorded on a dye record sheet along with a fiber sample of the dyeing for future reference.

Always record formulas as percentages instead of as volumes. A percentage can be used to calculate the volume required for any fiber weight, whereas a volume amount is valid only for the fiber weight of that dyeing. To convert a volume to a percent, divide the volume of the individual dye color by the total dye volume. For example, the formula for a dyeing that took 30 ml magenta and 10 ml turquoise to produce a 1% DOS for 40 g of fiber would be 75% magenta and 25% turquoise:

$$\frac{30 \text{ ml magenta}}{40 \text{ ml total volume}} \times 100 = 75\% \qquad \frac{10 \text{ ml turquoise}}{40 \text{ ml total volume}} \times 100 = 25\%$$

FORMULA 5

$$\% \text{ of color} = \frac{\text{volume of individual color}}{\text{total stock solution volume}} \times 100$$

---

[1]To convert a percent to a decimal, move the decimal point two places to the left.
  20% = 0.20   5% = 0.05   120% = 1.20

Volume of Water Used in the Dyebath

The volume of water used in the dyebath, referred to as the "dye liquor" must provide sufficient depth so that the fiber is completely immersed and able to move freely. These conditions allow the dye to be evenly distributed as it exhausts onto the fiber. Too much water, however, slows down the rate at which the dye exhausts and results in a lighter Depth of Shade within the prescribed time period of the dyeing. For results to be reproducible, the ratio of the weight of water to the weight of fiber (dye liquor ratio) must be constant.

Usually the dye liquor ratio is either 20:1 (20 weights water per weight of fiber) or 30:1 (30 weights water per weight of fiber). Refer to the dyeing procedure for the recommended ratio. With certain fibers such as silk which swells appreciably when wet, and some bulky yarns which take up more space in the dyebath, the dyer may want to increase the given dye liquor ratio if leveling is a problem.

The obvious question is how does the dyer measure a weight of water. In the metric system, 1 milliliter of water weighs 1 gram and occupies one cubic centimeter. This equivalency makes it possible to measure the weight of water as a volume. With a dye liquor ratio of 20:1, for example, the 20 weights of water become 20 milliliters of water per gram of fiber.

To calculate the total volume of water used in the dyepot, multiply the fiber weight times the dye liquor ratio. For example, with a dye liquor ratio of 30:1, it would take 3,600 ml of water in the dyepot to dye 120 grams of fiber.

$$\text{total volume of water} = 120 \text{ g} \times \frac{30 \text{ ml}}{1 \text{ g}} = 3{,}600 \text{ ml}$$

FORMULA 6
volume of water in dyebath = fiber weight × dye liquor ratio

A dyer using the U.S. system would have to convert the weight of water to a volume equivalent because there is no weight/volume equivalency. Since one gallon of water (128 ounces) weighs about 8 pounds, each weight amount must be divided by eight to determine the volume. For example, it would take 180 ounces (weight measurement) of water to dye six ounces of fiber at a 30:1 dye liquor ratio (formula 6).

$$\text{total weight of water} = 6 \text{ ounces} \times \frac{30}{1} = 180 \text{ ounces}$$

To convert 180 (weight) ounces to a volume equivalent, divide by 128 ounces (weight of 1 gallon of water) which gives 1.4 gallons of water.

$$\text{total volume of water} = \frac{180 \text{ ounces}}{128 \text{ ounces/gallon}} = 1.4 \text{ gallons}$$

The Dyeing Process

The actual dye procedures for the leveling acid and fiber-reactive dye series discussed in this book are based on industrial procedures but are geared to the methods available to the home dyer. A review of Chapters 3 and 4, The Protein Fiber Dyes and The Cellulose Fiber Dyes, will give the dyer a better understanding of why the various chemicals are used and the importance of following the procedures carefully. Refer to the material given in the first part of this chapter for additional information on performing the calculations.

For the other classes of dyes, follow the instructions provided by the distributor. With the background information presented in this book, the dyer should be able to perform any dyeing operation. Remember that the ability to match colors is one of the advantages of the synthetic dyes. This is only possible, though, if the dyer keeps accurate records, uses good laboratory techniques, follows directions carefully, and above all, is consistent.

Notes on the Leveling Acid Dyeing Procedure

Reproducible results do not depend on the precise measurement of the Glauber's salt and acetic acid. Small volumes of acid can be measured conveniently with a medicinal syringe. For larger amounts, a graduated cylinder or measuring cup can be used.

When dyeing color samples where the same fiber weight is used repeatedly, the Glauber's salt can be measured more easily with a teaspoon. First determine the volume of Glauber's salt by weighing it and then choose the size measuring spoon that would deliver a similar amount. If working with 10-gram fiber samples, for example, 20 percent Glauber's salt occupies a volume approximately the same as the amount measured by a quarter-teaspoon.

Acetic acid can be obtained from photo supply houses or camera shops. It is available in various concentrations, such as 96 percent, 56 percent and 28 percent. The quantity used in the dyeing procedure is based on 28 percent acetic acid. If the more concentrated solution (96 percent) is obtained, dilute using approximately 3.5 parts water to one part acid (volume of acid × 3.5 = volume of water) remembering to always *add acid to water*. If working with 56 percent acetic acid, use half the amount called for in the procedure.

Vinegar is approximately 5 percent acetic acid. It becomes an expensive ingredient when dyeing large quantities of fiber. Acetic acid is less expensive to use and does not permeate the room with vinegar fumes, an objectionable smell to some people.

The addition of the acetic acid enables the dye molecules to react chemically with the fiber. It is important to stir frequently, but gently, when the acid is first added for even dyeing results.

When working with wool, avoid excess movement of the fiber in the dyebath. The combination of heat, moisture and friction presents the ideal conditions for the felting of wool. Lift rather than stir the fiber. Because of the leveling ability of Glauber's salt, a minimum of stirring is usually needed to obtain streak-free dyeing.

Do not cut short the heating period. It is required to ensure the fastness properties of the dye.

It is important to wash the fiber following the dyeing process to remove the acetic acid, which if left in the fiber could weaken it.

Dyeing Protein Fibers Other Than Wool with the Leveling Acid Dyes

Being chemically similar to wool, the other protein fibers (for example, mohair, alpaca, cashmere and silk, as well as nylon, a synthetic fiber) react similarly with the acid dyes. This means the same dyeing procedure can be followed, with the few exceptions noted below.

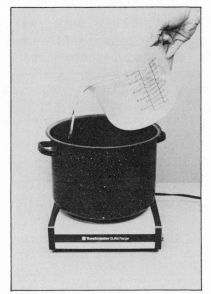

Step a.

Step c.

Step b.

Step d.

Leveling Acid Dyeing Procedure. *Step a.* Adding water to the dyepot. A large container with metric markings (illustrated) is useful for measuring large volumes of water.

Step b. A graduated cylinder is used to add the dyestock solutions to the dyebath. A pipette works well for measuring small volumes of dye solutions. Choose the equipment that most closely approximates the volume being measured.

Step c. Adding acetic acid to the dyebath. Either a syringe (illustrated) or a graduated cylinder can be used to measure acid. Either push the fiber to the side of the dyepot or remove it while the acid is being added.

Step d. After the dyeing procedure is completed, the dyebath should be neutralized (adjusted to a pH of 7) before pouring it down the drain. Broad-range pH paper is used to determine if the pH is neutral.

Because no two fibers are exactly alike, however, there is some variation in the color and the depth of color produced in the dyebath. If nylon, silk and wool are dyed at the same percent shade, the nylon will attain the darkest value, then the wool, with silk exhibiting the lightest color. Only by experimenting can the dyer determine how a particular fiber will react in comparison to wool.

Nylon

Fiber preparation with nylon is the same as with wool, except that the nylon does not need to be scoured unless obviously soiled. It still must be wetted, however. The dyeing process is basically the same as for wool, with the following exceptions: 1) Omit the Glauber's salt in the dyebath, since with nylon it does not aid the leveling process. Nylon is more prone to streaking than wool and may require the use of special leveling agents. 2) Use a hotter temperature (boiling) and a longer reaction time (one hour) than with wool. 3) Stir frequently to encourage leveling while gradually raising the temperature.

Silk

When preparing silk for the dyebath, follow the same procedure as for wool, including the scouring process. The same dyeing process is also used, except that the temperature of the dyebath should be raised slowly to a maximum of 185° F. and not allowed to go any higher. Boiling will weaken the silk and reduce its luster. Although silk does not obtain as deep a color as wool at the same concentration of dye, it is more reactive; the dye is capable of bonding with the fiber at temperatures as low as 105° F. As a result, it is not necessary to keep the dyebath as hot.

When working with silk, handle the fiber carefully; it is especially prone to tangling when wet. Using extra ties (a minimum of four or five) with the skeins will help to keep them in order. One method that can be used to minimize tangling in the dyebath is to place a rod across the top of the dyepot. Slip a long cord over the rod with the other end attached to the skein so that the silk can still be completely immersed in the dyebath. By raising and lowering the rod, the silk can be moved with a minimum of

TABLE 24

LEVELING ACID DYEING PROCEDURE

Ingredients	Volume of warm water (110° F) +	Weight of Glauber's salt (g) +	Volume of 1% dyestock sol. (ml)
Amount	fiber weight (g) × dye liquor ratio (30 ml water per g fiber)	fiber weight (g) × 20%	fiber weight (g) × Depth of Shade × percent of color
Procedure	Add water, salt and dyestock solution to the dyepot and mix well. Add the wetted fiber (squeeze out excess water) and raise the temperature of the dyebath over a 15 minute period to 170°-180° F. Stir frequently to insure even penetration of the fiber with the dyestock solution.		

ADD

Ingredient	Volume of 28% acetic acid (ml)
Amount	fiber weight (g) × 10%
Procedure	Push fiber to one side of dyepot, or remove it and add the appropriate volume of acetic acid. Stir well. Replace the fiber and continue raising the temperature of the dyebath approximately 200°-212° F. (heat to 185°-190° F. for silk; for nylon, heat to boiling). Hold at this temperature for 45 minutes, stirring occasionally.
Finishing	Allow the fiber to cool, then wash with a neutral detergent (for example, Ivory Liquid). Rinse well and remove excess water by spinning fiber in washing machine. Dry fiber out of direct sunlight.

tangling. Be sure to alter the position of the ties occasionally. Even if loosely tied, they may cause a tie-dye effect.

For certain chemical reasons, the leveling acid dyes do not produce as successful dyeing results with silk as they do with the other protein fibers. In fact, some dyes—red, magenta, yellow and blue—do not appreciably react at all. Lemon yellow, turquoise, sapphire blue and scarlet can be substituted for these colors, although the color mixing range will be altered (see photos on page 27). In general, silk dyes lighter and has poorer washfastness with the leveling acid dyes than does wool.

Industrially, various dye classes are used for the production of specific colors on silk, with no one class of dyes able to provide satisfactory results for all the colors. The super milling (neutral acid) dyes and the 1:2 premetallized dyes give the best overall results, although the colors are not as bright with the premetallized dyes and level dyeing is more difficult to achieve.

Notes on the Fiber-Reactive Dyeing Procedures

The dyeing procedures given by the various distributors for the fiber-reactive dyes may differ from those presented here. Regardless of the method used, it is important that enough salt be added to allow maximum adsorption of the dye by the fiber, and enough alkali to raise the pH above 10 so that the dye reaction can properly occur. The amount of salt and/or alkali can be reduced if the dyer determines through experimentation that no visible loss of color occurs. On the other hand, these amounts should be increased if the dyer finds that a greater depth of color can be achieved. For color matching purposes, the dyer should adopt one procedure and stick with it. Do not vary the percentages of salt and alkali or the reaction process, or color results will vary. Be consistent!

The washing soda sold in the grocery store should not be used with the fiber-reactive dyes; additives in the product interfere with the dye reaction. Instead, purchase the washing soda from distributors who sell the dye.

Dyeing requires large quantities of salt. An economical way to buy it is in five-pound bags sold in grocery stores for pickling.

The percentages of salt and alkali given in the dyeing procedures are based on a 20:1 dye liquor ratio. For this reason it is important to measure the water accurately. If a larger volume of water than 20:1 is added to the dyebath, it will lower the concentration of salt and alkali, which will in turn reduce the depth of color.

The fiber-reactive dyes are not sensitive to hard water, but minerals in it can precipitate when the washing soda is added, causing a deposit on the fiber. This reaction can also remove some of the alkali, resulting in a lower pH and consequently weaker shades. To determine whether a water softener is necessary, compare a sample dyed using tap water with one using distilled water. If there is a noticeable difference in color, a water softener, such as Calgon, should be added.

TABLE 25

PROCION MX DYEING PROCEDURE

Ingredients	Volume of warm water (105° F)	Weight of salt (g)
Amounts	fiber weight (g) × dye liquor ratio (20 ml water per g fiber)	fiber weight (g) × percent of salt*
Procedure	Add salt and water to dyepot and mix to dissolve. Enter previously scoured (boiled 30 minutes with Synthrapol) and wetted fiber, squeeze out excess water and stir occasionally over a 10-minute period.	

ADD

Ingredient	Volume of 1% dyestock sol. (ml)
Amount	fiber weight (g) × Depth of Shade × % of color
Procedure	Either remove the fiber, or push it to one side of dyepot, and add dyestock solution. Stir well. Reenter the fiber, if previously removed, and stir frequently over a 30-minute period.

ADD

Ingredient	Weight of washing soda (g)
Amount	fiber weight (g) × 10%
Procedure	Dissolve washing soda in small amount of warm water. Push fiber to the side of dyepot and add soda. Stir well, and soak at room temperature (not above 105° F) for 45 minutes with frequent stirring.
Finishing	Rinse fiber in cold water. Wash with Synthrapol (½-1 tsp/gal of water) or other scouring agent at temperature of 190° F to boil for 10 minutes. Rinse fiber with warm water, remove excess water and dry.

*The weight of salt is dependent on the Depth of Shade. As the amount of dye is increased, more salt is required.

Depth of Shade	% Salt
up to 0.5%	20%
0.5%-2.0%	50%
2.0%-4.0%	90%
above 4.0%	110% or greater

The amount of stirring required to obtain even dye results varies with the dye series and the type of material being dyed. Fabric, for example, requires more stirring than yarns because it

TABLE 26

CIBACRON F DYEING PROCEDURE

Ingredients	Volume of warm water (105° F) +	Weight of salt (g) +	Volume of 1% dyestock sol. (ml)
Amount	fiber weight (g) × dye liquor ratio (20 ml water per g fiber)	fiber weight (g) × percent of salt*	fiber weight (g) × Depth of Shade × percent of color
Procedure	Add salt and dye to the water in dyepot and mix well. Enter the previously scoured (boiled 30 minutes with Synthrapol) and wetted fiber, squeeze out excess water, and stir. Raise dyebath temperature to 140° F and hold for 45 minutes, with frequent stirring.		

ADD

Ingredient	Weight of washing soda (g)
Amount	fiber weight (g) × 10%
Procedure	Dissolve washing soda in small amount of warm water. Either remove fiber or push fiber to side of dyebath and add soda. Stir well and re-enter fiber if previously removed. Continue holding temperature at 140° F for 45 minutes with frequent stirring.
Finishing	Rinse fiber thoroughly in cold water until water runs clear. Wash fiber with Synthrapol (½-1 tsp/gal of water) or other scouring agent at a temperature of 190° F to boil for 10 minutes. Rinse fiber in warm water, remove excess water, and dry.

*The weight of salt is dependent on the Depth of Shade. As the amount of dye is increased, more salt is required.

Depth of Shade	% Salt
up to 0.5%	60%
0.5%-2.0%	90%
2.0%-4.0%	120%
above 4%	140%

forms folds and creases in the dyepot. Additional stirring is needed to penetrate these areas, especially when the dye and the alkali are first added, because most of the dye reaction occurs at this time. If dye results are uneven, more frequent stirring is needed.

When dyeing multiple dyebaths of small amounts of fiber (for example, color samples) it is more convenient to add the washing soda as a solution using a syringe instead of weighing out and

TABLE 27

PROCION H & HE DYEING PROCEDURE

Ingredients	Volume of warm water (105° F) +	Weight of salt (g) +	Volume of 1% dyestock sol. (ml)
Amount	fiber weight (g) × dye liquor ratio (20 ml water per g fiber)	fiber weight (g) × percent of salt*	fiber weight (g) × Depth of Shade × percent of color
Procedure	Add the salt and dye to the water and stir to mix well. Add the wetted fiber (squeeze out excess water) and raise the temperature of the dyebath to 175° F. Stir frequently over a 20-minute period at this temperature.		

ADD

Ingredient	Weight of washing soda (g)
Amount	fiber weight (g) × 30%
Procedure	Dissolve the washing soda in small amount of warm water and add to the dyebath. Stir well. Continue stirring occasionally over a 45-minute period, keeping the temperature of the dyebath at 175° F.
Finishing	Rinse the fiber thoroughly in cold water. Wash with Synthrapol or other scouring agent at a boil for 10 minutes. Rinse the fiber with several short baths of hot water until clear. The fiber can be spun in the washing machine to remove excess water.

*The weight of salt used in the dyebath is dependent on the Depth of Shade. As the amount of dye is increased, more salt is required.

Depth of Shade	% Salt
up to 0.5% (pale)	80%
0.5%-2.0% (light to medium)	120%
2.0%-4.0% (medium to dark)	150%
above 4% (deep)	200%

dissolving the soda for each dyebath. This is accomplished by preparing a stock solution of washing soda.

A 25 percent stock solution of washing soda is made by placing 25 grams of the powder in a container and adding enough hot water to bring the volume up to 100 milliliters. More concentrated solutions are not recommended because it is difficult to dissolve all of the alkali. Even a 25 percent solution should be kept warm while in use or the soda will settle out.

To determine the volume of 25 percent stock solution to add to the dyebath, first calculate how many grams of washing soda are needed. Then divide this figure by the grams of washing soda contained in each milliliter of the 25 percent stock solution which is 0.25 grams per milliliter. For example, if the dyeing procedure calls for 3 grams of washing soda, it would take 12 milliliters of the 25 percent stock solution to yield this weight of soda.

$$\text{Total volume of 25\% stock solution} = \frac{3 \text{ g washing soda}}{0.25 \text{ g washing soda/ml 25\% stock}} = 12 \text{ ml 25\% stock}$$

The fiber-reactive dyes require special handling to remove all of the unfixed dye and thus ensure optimum fastness. Synthrapol, a commercial scouring product, is designed for this purpose, using ½ to 1 teaspoon per gallon of water. The fiber should be soaped at a temperature of 190° F. to the boil for a period of 10 minutes to be certain that all of the unfixed dye is removed. For the chemical reasons explained in Chapter 4, several short rinsings in hot water after soaping are preferable to one long rinse for removing all of the unfixed dye.

When dyeing large quantities of fabric with the "cold" type fiber-reactive dyes, any plastic container such as a wastebasket or even a child's plastic swimming pool can be used as a dyepot. The washing machine also works quite successfully. Choose a container shape deep enough so that the fabric can be easily stirred.

Notes on the Cibacron F Dyeing Procedure

The Cibacron F dyes were designed for use with caustic soda, a chemical that is unsafe for most dyers to work with in the home. Instead, most home dyers use washing soda. While this product is safer to work with, it does not create as alkaline a dyebath as the caustic soda and the dyes are not able to work as effectively. Improved results can be obtained, however, by running the dyebath at 140° F. instead of 105° F. At the higher temperature, the dyes more easily penetrate the fiber, and both leveling and dye yield are improved. If a heat source is not available, use hot (120° F.) tap water. Also, when dyeing silk with the Cibacron F dyes, do not raise the temperature above 120° F.

9. Gradations

Nature as a Source for Color Mixing Ideas

Nature can be the dyer's best source of inspiration for color combinations. A study of nature in the field or through colored photographs in magazines, books or calendars provides countless ideas for colors to be used together. Many unusual color effects can be derived from these sources, and color play and movement combining subtle tones with bold accents can be observed.

Close examination of a sunset, for example, will reveal the many tints and tones of a few key colors that are combined to give such a striking display. And the colors created when sunlight reflects off a pool of water present a contrast of highlights and shadows using a limited number of colors.

The dyer can capture the colors of nature in fibers and recreate many of her exciting color efforts. First, however, the dyer must study color mixing effects to learn how the dyes interact, and become familiar with the colors that can be produced in the dyepot using just the primary hues. Only with the knowledge that comes from studying color mixing can the dyer creatively work with the dyes.

Importance of Gradations

Gradations offer the dyer a useful method for systematically exploring color mixing effects. A *gradation* is a series of colors exhibiting a regular degree of change in one particular dimension such as hue, intensity or value. If enough steps are included in the gradation, then the color movement becomes so gradual that

123

all the colors appear to flow together. Combining blue with yellow in various amounts will produce a gradation of hues from yellow-green through green to green-blue. Varying the amounts of dye from just a small amount to a large quantity will give a value gradation from a pale tint to a color of full intensity. The addition of increasing amounts of violet to yellow will create a gradation of shades of reduced intensity.

A gradation of colors can be obtained by systematically mixing: 1) two primary colors, 2) a color in varying amounts of stock solution or 3) two or more colors that produce a tertiary shade. In this way the three dimensions of color can be studied. The first method provides a means for examining hue effects, the second for studying the value scale of colors and the third for exploring the intensity range of colors.

By mixing colors in a methodical way, the dyer can produce a series of colors whose relationship to each other is obvious. With gradations, color movement can be studied as the range of mixed colors possible from two or more parent colors is demonstrated visually. This knowledge is especially beneficial in understanding the composition of mixed colors. Mixing red with green in varying amounts produces a range of shades from dull red through the browns to the dull greens. It is hard to imagine that red and green mixed together can produce a lovely brown, but it is possible. The visual impact of seeing this is such that the next time this particular shade of brown is seen its composition will be recognized.

In addition to the knowledge gained from exploring color mixing, the dyer also obtains a stock of dyed color samples which provide invaluable information for formulating other colors. Because the samples show a regular movement of color, it is possible through comparative matching to develop dye formulas for unknown colors. For example, if a color to be mixed lies between two colors whose formulas are 10 percent color A plus 90 percent color B and 20 percent color A plus 80 percent color B, then the unknown formula must contain between 10 percent and 20 percent color A and between 80 and 90 percent color B. Trial blends are necessary to obtain the exact color match, but because of the information provided by the color samples the dyer has a logical place to begin. If, instead, the dyer had only a randomly-obtained selection of dye samples, it would be hard to determine which colors shared a common background.

In performing a gradation series for the purpose of obtaining dye samples, the number of steps included will depend on the degree of color change desired. From a practical point of view, however, some limit to the amount of dyeing is necessary. Aim for a smooth transition of color without including any more steps than are necessary.

With hue and intensity gradations, a smooth transition can usually be accomplished using ten to twelve steps when going from one color to another (such as from red to yellow or from red to green). With a value gradation, fewer steps are needed: seven steps will provide a smooth transition of color from very pale to quite dark.

Some hue and complement series require more steps than others because of the value differences inherent in the hues. A color of high value like yellow, for example, will be significantly altered by the addition of just a small amount of a color of low value such as blue. On the other hand, two colors of similar value, such as red and green, do not have as great an effect on each other, so that fewer steps are needed to produce a smooth transition of color.

Hue Gradation

Hue gradations provide a method for obtaining all of the intermediate and secondary hues found on the color wheel by mixing two primary colors in a systematic way. If the gradation includes enough steps, the color movement around the wheel is so subtle that the colors blend together. For the reasons mentioned above, however, ten to twelve steps are usually sufficient to obtain samples of adjacent colors for color matching purposes.

The following example (Table 28) of a hue gradation from yellow to red illustrates the number of steps that are needed to provide a smooth transition of color. The percent shade of the dyeing depends on the needs of the dyer although both a 1 percent shade (medium value) and a 0.1 percent shade (pale value) are useful for providing a moderately intense and a pale range of shades. The pale shades are useful because it is often difficult to visualize how an intense color will appear at a much lighter value.

In the above gradation the darker color (red) was added to the lighter color (yellow), beginning with very small quantities of the red. A very small volume of red dye solution added to yellow

TABLE 28

YELLOW TO RED HUE GRADATION

Weight of fiber: 10 grams
Stock solution strength: 1%
Formula: Fiber weight × (% of color) × (% shade)

PERCENT YELLOW	AMOUNT OF YELLOW STOCK SOLUTION		PERCENT RED	AMOUNT OF RED STOCK SOLUTION	
	1% SHADE	0.1% SHADE		1% SHADE	0.1% SHADE
99%	9.9 mls	0.99 mls	1%	0.1 ml	0.01 ml
97.5%	9.75 mls	0.98 mls	2.5%	0.25 mls	0.02 mls
95%	9.5 mls	0.95 mls	5%	0.5 mls	0.05 mls
90%	9.0 mls	0.9 mls	10%	1.0 mls	0.1 ml
80%	8.0 mls	0.8 mls	20%	2.0 mls	0.2 mls
70%	7.0 mls	0.7 mls	30%	3.0 mls	0.3 mls
60%	6.0 mls	0.6 mls	40%	4.0 mls	0.4 mls
50%	5.0 mls	0.5 mls	50%	5.0 mls	0.5 mls
40%	4.0 mls	0.4 mls	60%	6.0 mls	0.6 mls
30%	3.0 mls	0.3 mls	70%	7.0 mls	0.7 mls
20%	2.0 mls	0.2 mls	80%	8.0 mls	0.8 mls
10%	1.0 mls	0.1 mls	90%	9.0 mls	0.9 mls

produces an orange cast. As the mixture approaches red, however, the red so totally dominates the blend that the yellow produces no significant color change. As a result, there is no need to include additional steps using smaller amounts of yellow. The number of steps is determined by the color effects that are produced.

Mixed Secondary Colors

By visually comparing the colors produced by the hue gradation series with the hues on the color wheel, the formulas for the major secondary colors—green, orange and violet—are determined. As explained in Chapter 5, the variations that exist between the actual dyes and the theoretical colors on which the color wheel is based are responsible for the fact that two primary dyes used to mix a secondary color are not combined in the expected 50:50 ratio. Table 29 gives the actual percentages of each primary that can be blended to produce the mixed secondary colors with the leveling acid dyes. The secondary colors produced with red, yellow and blue are of different intensities than

TABLE 29

MIXED LEVELING ACID SECONDARY COLORS

10% red + 90% yellow = orange
10% magenta + 90% yellow = orange
30% blue + 70% yellow = green
20% turquoise + 80% yellow = green
40% red + 60% blue = violet
80% magenta + 20% turquoise = violet

those obtained using magenta, turquoise and yellow. However, both sets of secondary colors are important for mixing purposes.

This information is important because it allows the dyer to mix the secondary colors instead of buying the secondary dyes. As a result, the dyer needs to stock only the five primary dyestuffs to mix most other colors. If, for example, a leveling acid dye formula calls for mixing 30 percent yellow with 70 percent violet, the dyer may substitute red and blue (or magenta and turquoise) dyestock solutions for the violet. According to the above formulas for the secondary colors, the violet to be used is composed of 40 percent red and 60 percent blue. To calculate the percentages of red and blue that are to be substituted for the violet, multiply the percentage of violet used in the formula times the percentage of each of the two primary colors which combine to make up violet:

70% violet × 40% red = 28% red
70% violet × 60% blue = 42% blue

Thus the dyer achieves the same color called for in the original formula (30 percent yellow + 70 percent violet) by mixing 30 percent yellow with 28 percent red and 42 percent blue. The only difference is that the color produced using only the primary dyestock solutions will be of a lower intensity than if the secondary dyes had been used (see Chapter 5).

Value Gradations

A value gradation is used to produce a range of colors from very pale to deep. By simply increasing or decreasing the total volume

A seven-step value gradation gives a smooth transition of color movement from very pale to quite deep.

of stock solution, every primary, secondary and tertiary color can be blended to give lighter or darker values. As already mentioned, the number of steps is less important than the achievement of a smooth transition of color from light to dark. What is a very light color to one person may not be to another. Therefore, each dyer should include the number of steps considered necessary.

Table 30 illustrates how a value gradation series is performed.

Complement Gradation

Colors that are opposite each other on the color wheel are called complements. Adding one complement to another has the effect of graying or darkening that color because any pair of complements contains some proportion of all three primaries. (Remember that the subtractive theory of color states that when equal amounts of red, yellow and blue are added together black is formed. See Chapter 5.)

Complement gradations provide the dyer with a method of mixing vibrant shades without using black. Colors grayed with a complement appear more "alive" than the same colors grayed with black. Tones are similarly produced by adding some of a color's complement to the tint of that color. For example, a small amount of green added to pink—a tint of red—will produce a beige tone. Again, this is the preferred method for graying a color.

The major pairs of complements are: 1) red-green, 2) yellow-violet and 3) blue-orange. Remember, however, that any two

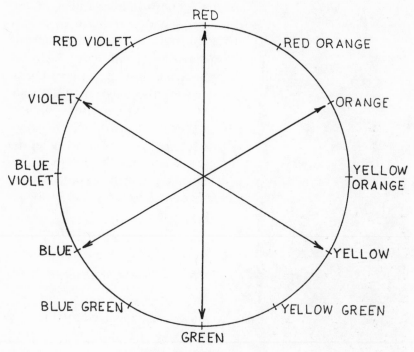

RED

RED VIOLET

RED ORANGE

VIOLET

ORANGE

BLUE
VIOLET

YELLOW
ORANGE

BLUE

YELLOW

BLUE GREEN

YELLOW GREEN

GREEN

24. Major complementary color pairs.

colors opposite each other on the wheel are considered complements, and a mixture of each pair produces a different range of tertiary shades. It is for this reason that complement gradations provide an important method for mixing a wide range of tertiary colors.

Although a complement gradation involves the mixing of just two dye colors, it is actually a three-color blend. This is because one or both of the complementary colors are mixtures of two other colors, so that the three primary colors are always present. For example, when mixing red with its complement green, the dyer is really combining red with a constant percentage of yellow and blue. While the percentages of red and green dyes change in the gradation, the percentage composition of green (for example, 30 percent blue + 70 percent yellow) always remains the same.

This allows the color movement to progress in a linear direction across the color wheel.

As explained in Chapter 5, all complement gradations pass through the center area of the color wheel. This means that each complementary pair is capable of producing a range of browns, providing a very effective method for mixing these shades. The red-green series, for example, produces a range of red-browns and green-browns, while the yellow-violet series produces the yellow-browns and the violet-browns.

Table 31 illustrates how a complement gradation series is performed.

A value gradation was used very effectively to create this handsome blue jacket woven by Lynn Hanson from yarns dyed by Kathy Sylvan. Photo courtesy of Kathy Sylvan.

Three-Color Mixtures

The gradations considered so far have involved mixing just two dye colors at any one time, for example, red and yellow or red and green. It is also possible to obtain a gradation of colors by systematically mixing three primary colors. This is referred to as a trichromatic blend and is especially valuable for producing a large number of tertiary colors.

The system is based on a certain total number of parts, such as ten; the sum of the proportions of the three primary colors composing the mixture always equals this number. The proportions of the three parts are altered in a systematic fashion until all the possible three-number combinations equalling the total number have been used. The larger the total number of parts, the greater the number of tertiary shades and the more gradual the movement of color, but for the mathematical reasons explained later, a ten-part system is easiest to work with.

Every dye formula is composed of three numbers, each representing a proportion of a particular dye color, with the sum of the
three numbers equalling the total number of parts. The first

TABLE 30

RED VALUE GRADATION SERIES

Weight of fiber: 10 grams
Stock solution strength: 1%
Percent of color: 100% (unmixed color)
Formula: Fiber weight × (% of color) × (% shade)

VALUE RANGE	AMOUNT OF 1% STOCK SOLUTION	PERCENT SHADE
Very Pale	1.0 ml	0.1%
Pale	2.5 mls	0.25%
Pastel	5.0 mls	0.5%
Light-Medium	10 mls	1.0%
Medium	20 mls	2.0%
Medium-Dark	30 mls	3.0%
Deep	40 mls	4.0%

number in the formula refers to color A, the second to color B and
the third to color C. For example, with a ten-part system a dye
formula expressed as 721 (read as "seven, two, one," not "seven

TABLE 31

RED-GREEN COMPLEMENT GRADATION

Weight of fiber: 10 grams
Stock solution strength: 1%
Percent shade: 1% or light-medium
Formula: Fiber-weight × (% of color) × (% shade)

PERCENT RED	AMOUNT OF RED STOCK SOLUTION	PERCENT GREEN	AMOUNT OF GREEN STOCK SOLUTION
95%	9.5 mls	5%	0.5 mls
90%	9.0 mls	10%	1.0 mls
80%	8.0 mls	20%	2.0 mls
70%	7.0 mls	30%	3.0 mls
60%	6.0 mls	40%	4.0 mls
50%	5.0 mls	50%	5.0 mls
40%	4.0 mls	60%	6.0 mls
30%	3.0 mls	70%	7.0 mls
20%	2.0 mls	80%	8.0 mls
10%	1.0 mls	90%	9.0 mls
5%	.05 mls	95%	9.5 mls

hundred twenty-one") refers to a mixed color composed of seven
parts color A, two parts color B and one part color C. Another

color represented as 253 contains two parts color A, five parts color B and three parts color C. If only two primary colors are involved in the mixture, the absent primary color is represented by zero. For example, 091 refers to a color which contains zero parts color A, nine parts color B and one part color C.

When mixing a particular color, the dyer must first convert the number of parts into percentages so that the volume of dye

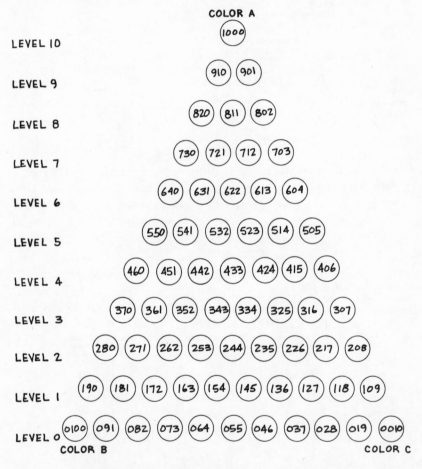

25. Trichromatic color mixing system based on ten parts.

solution can be calculated for a particular fiber weight. A ten-part system simplifies the conversion; all that is necessary is to multiply each of the parts by ten. The color mentioned above—721—

contains 70 percent color A, 20 percent color B and 10 percent color C. By referring to the formula given in Chapter 8 for calculating the volume of dye solution, the dyer can easily determine the amounts of stock solution needed for the particular fiber weight.

Diagram 25 illustrates a three-color system based on ten total parts. The orderly change in the number of parts provides a systematic method for mixing tertiary colors.

The points of the triangle represent the three primary colors, with colors B (0100) and C (0010) the base colors and color A (1000) located at the apex of the triangle. The triangle is divided into different levels, with the number of levels determined by the total number of parts. For example, with the ten-part system shown in the diagram there are 11 levels going from 0 through 10. At each level, color C is systematically increased going from left to right while color B is systematically decreased going in the same direction, with color A remaining static for that level. Color A increases numerically from bottom to top with the particular level reflecting the number of parts of this color. For example, the bottom level ("0") represents zero parts of color A, indicating that all the colors on this level are two-color blends.

All of the colors located on the outside legs of the triangle are two-color blends and all of the three-color mixtures are located within the triangle. As with the color wheel, the location of a color in the triangle reflects the percentage composition of the three primary colors which produce it. The positions of the colors also reflect their intensity: the more intense two-color blends are located on the outer rim of the triangle while the less intense tertiary colors are located inside. The degree of intensity decreases as the colors move towards the center area of the triangle (black), with the three colors 433, 343, and 334 exhibiting the lowest intensity. This is because their composition is approaching that of an equal blend, the formula for black.

10. Where to Begin

The Importance of Dye Color Samples

The obvious question of each new synthetic dyer is "How much of a particular dye do I mix with another to obtain a certain shade?" The frustrating answer is "Experiment to find out." While it is possible to give dye formulas for mixing various colors in a particular dye series, the information is of limited value because the name used to describe the mixed color does not mean the same thing to each individual. If, for example, the dyer was told that one part of Procion Turquoise MX-G mixed with an equal amount of Procion Yellow MX-8G would produce "kelly green," it would still be necessary to produce this color to see how it actually appears.

For this reason, it is important for every dyer to develop his or her own inventory of color samples for which the dye formulas are known. A useful basic stock of colors from known formulas should include: samples in both a medium and a pale shade for each hue of the various color wheels; their major complement gradations; and the tertiary shades produced by mixing three primary colors in a ten-or-more-part system (see Chapter 9, "Gradations").

Samples of both an intense and a pale value of a color are important to the dyer because it is sometimes difficult to guess visually how an intense shade will appear as a tint. Often the parentage of an intense color is more obvious when it becomes lighter. A shade of violet, for example, could favor either the blue or the red parent. In a lighter value this can be determined more easily as the red or the blue comes to dominate the mixture.

Every dyer should first determine the percent shades at which to dye his or her color samples. For this reason, a value gradation of the primary hues of each dye class should be performed first. Because of the simplified mathematical calculations a 1 percent and a 0.1 percent shade are easy values to work with, although more intense shades may be preferred with some of the dye series. This is a personal decision. There will be some variation within each dye class in the intensity of a particular dye at a certain percent shade. For example, with the leveling acid dyes, a 1 percent shade of magenta will produce a more intense color than a 1 percent shade of red. To simplify the procedure of obtaining color samples, however, it is easier to dye all of the samples at the same percent shades within a series.

By dyeing small quantities and working with mill end wool yarns and inexpensive cotton twine or fabric, the cost of obtaining color samples can be kept to a minimum. Ten-gram (about one-third-ounce) skeins of yarn or fabric are adequate. Although quite small volumes of dyestock solution are involved when dyeing pale shades, a one-ml pipette makes it possible to measure these amounts accurately.

The importance of these color samples cannot be overemphasized. They are invaluable as a reference standard for making color decisions and for formulating other colors. A dyer's color samples provide an insight into how the dyes interact and the color ranges that can be produced by mixing two or more colors together. They are the key to unlocking the door to color mixing.

Multiple Dyebaths

It takes approximately one to one and one-half hours to complete a dyeing procedure regardless of the amount of fiber being dyed. Hence experienced dyers run several dyebaths at once. The main consideration is having extra dyepots and heat sources (not necessary with the "cold" fiber-reactive dyes). With a four-burner stove, a dyer can run four dyepots; if hot plates are used in addition, it is possible to dye even more yarns at one time.

For dyeing small amounts of fiber (20 grams or less) such as for color samples, a canning kettle with jars can provide a multiple dyebath setup. Each jar serves as an individual dyepot, making it possible to run seven samples at one time. For each additional canning kettle, another seven samples can be dyed in the same time span. It is also possible for several people to divide the job of dyeing color samples and then share the results. This further

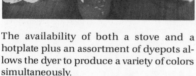

The availability of both a stove and a hotplate plus an assortment of dyepots allows the dyer to produce a variety of colors simultaneously.

A multiple dyebath set-up showing canning jars used as individual dyepots.

reduces the amount of time spent developing samples. Regardless of how the samples are obtained, they are a necessary tool for all future dyeing work.

When measuring the dyes for a multiple dyebath setup, pipette one dyestock solution at a time for all of the dyebaths or jars being prepared instead of adding all of the dye colors to one dyebath before going on to the next. In this way the pipette does not have to be rinsed until the dyer is completely finished with a particular color.

Availability of the Dyes

Some dye series are available through a large number of distributors, while others are carried by only a few and, in some cases, by just one retail outlet. Because the fiber-reactive dyes are widely used for so many dyeing techniques (batiking and silk-screening, to name only two), many dealers specialize in stocking them. A list of supply sources, current at time of publication, is included in the Appendix to aid the dyer in locating these outlets.

Because the various distributors obtain their dyes from different wholesalers, not every distributor will have the same selection or type of dyes. The availability of a particular dye may also change for a variety of reasons: it may be replaced by an improved dye, or discontinued by the manufacturer for economic reasons. In such cases, check with the distributor to determine what replacement will most closely approximate the old color. (Remember that whenever a different color is substituted, color mixing results will be altered.) New advancements and changes are continually being made in the dye industry, and home dyers should try to keep informed of those developments that pertain to their work. Some distributors provide their customers with this service through newsletters or bulletins.

Which Dyes to Purchase

In each of the dye series, certain colors are particularly useful for mixing other shades. These dyes are considered the "primaries," and are selected because they closely approximate the primaries on which the color wheel is based. The closer the dye matches a color wheel primary, the greater the color mixing range. Occasionally, a color that is not a primary, such as navy blue or golden yellow, is also selected to facilitate color mixing. While other colors are generally available to the home dyer for each of the dye series, it becomes expensive to buy all of them, especially when similar shades can be mixed using a basic stock of colors. It is not necessary to tie up a large amount of money in dye inventory.

Importance of the C.I. Name When Purchasing the Acid Dyes

Because the patents for most of the acid dyes expired some time ago, any given generic color is likely to be available today under a variety of commercial names. Table 32 shows the many commercial names under which the generic dye Acid Yellow 17 is marketed.

As the preceding table illustrates, the C.I. generic name and not the brand name of a dye is what is important. To the home dyer it really doesn't matter whose brand is used.

Furthermore, a general color description such as "yellow" is not sufficient, since a dye manufacturer often produces a wide range of a particular color. The range of yellow dyes produced by Ciba-Geigy is demonstrated in Table 33.

In addition, the various distributors do not always describe a color in the same terms. Without the benefit of a color sample it is

TABLE 32

MANUFACTURERS OF ACID YELLOW 17*

MANUFACTURER	COMMERCIAL NAME
Harshaw Chemical Co.	Acracid Fast Light Yellow 2G
Benzenoid Organics, Inc.	Benzorco Fast Light Yellow 2G
Berncolors-Poughkeepsie, Inc.	Bernacid Yellow 2GLX
American Cyanamid Co.	Calcocid Fast Yellow 2G Super
Ciba-Geigy Corp.	Erio Fast Flavine 3G Supra
Ciba-Geigy Corp.	Erio Yellow 2G
Ciba-Geigy Corp.	Erio Flavine 3G
Nyanza Inc.	Fast Light Yellow 2G
Hilton-Davis Chemical Co.	Hidacid Light Yellow 2G
Crompton & Knowles	Intracid Fast Yellow 2GC
Crompton & Knowles	Intracid Fast Yellow 2GL
Verona Dyestuff Division	Levalan Yellow GG
ICI	Lissamine Yellow 2G125
Harshaw Chemical Co.	Neutral Brilliant Yellow 3GLL
Organic Chemical Corp.	Orcoacid Fast Light Yellow 2G
Sandoz Colors & Chemicals	Xylene Light Yellow 2G

*Source: *Journal of the American Association of Textile Chemists and Colorists*, Vol. 8, No. 7A (July 1976)

not possible for the user to tell whether the yellows described in two different catalogs are identical. By knowing the C.I. name, however, the dyer can determine this information.

TABLE 33

LEVELING ACID YELLOW DYES PRODUCED BY CIBA-GEIGY*

COMMERCIAL NAME	C.I. GENERIC NAME
Yellow 2G	Acid Yellow 17
Yellow 7GF	Acid Yellow 3
Yellow 2GLN	Acid Yellow 169
Yellow 3GRL	Acid Yellow 10
Yellow 3GS	Acid Yellow 29
Yellow 4R	Acid Yellow 219
Yellow RLS	Acid Yellow 25
Yellow T Supra	Acid Yellow 23
Yellow S	Acid Yellow 27

*Taken from *Colour Index*

Acid Dye Inventory

The C.I. names listed below for the leveling acid and premetallized dyes represent those most commonly available to the home

TABLE 34

BASIC INVENTORY FOR ACID DYES

GENERAL COLOR DESCRIPTION	C.I. NAME
ACID LEVELING DYES	
Red	Acid Red 1
Yellow	Acid Yellow 17
Bright Blue	Acid Blue 45
Turquoise	Acid Blue 9
Magenta	Acid Violet 7
Black	none
For Use With Silk:	
Scarlet	Acid Red 73
Lemon Yellow	Acid Yellow 23
Sapphire Blue	Acid Blue 7
PREMETALLIZED DYES	
Bright Red	Acid Red 211
Brilliant Blue*	Acid Red 183
Brilliant Yellow*	Acid Yellow 127
Black	Acid Black 107

*Super milling dyes. Colors are brighter than the premetallized dyes with the same high washfastness property.

dyer. If dealing with a distributor who carries other C.I. colors, ask for the shop's recommendations in selecting the primaries. Table 34 gives a suggested list of acid dyes to be used as primaries for color mixing.

Purchasing the Fiber-Reactive Dyes

It is important to know the generic names when purchasing the acid dyes to identify which commercial names are chemically identical. Unlike the acid dyes, however, many of the fiber-reactive dyes are still protected by patents. In such cases no company may chemically duplicate another company's dyes. For this reason it is not necessary to use the generic name when purchasing the reactive dyes since they are chemically unique. Instead, the company's commercial name, such as "Procion Red MX-5B," is adequate.

As with the acid dyes, however, the use of a general color description such as "red" is not sufficient, since many similar

TABLE 35

PROCION MX FIBER-REACTIVE RED DYES

COMMERCIAL NAME	COLOR DESCRIPTION USED BY VARIOUS DISTRIBUTORS						
	Cerulean Blue	Keystone-Ingham	Pylam	Fabdec	Dharma	Textile Resources	Flynns
Red MX-5B		Bright Red	Brilliant Bluish				Fire Engine Red
Red MX-8B	Fuchsia	Brilliant Red	Magenta	Cool Red	Fuchsia	Fuchsia	Fuchsia Red
Red MX-BA	Carmine Red		Chinese				
Red MX-BCA		Red	Chinese			Bright Red	
Red MX-G			True				
Scarlet MX-BA	Bright Scarlet		Bright		Fire Engine Red		
Scarlet MX-2BA			Brighter				
Scarlet MX-BRA			Brilliant	Scarlet			
Scarlet MX-G		Scarlet	Bluish	Warm Red	Scarlet		Scarlet

colors may be produced by the same company. To compound the confusion, the various distributors' catalogs may use the same color description for several different reds, or may use different

TABLE 36

BASIC INVENTORY FOR CIBACRON F FIBER-REACTIVE DYES

COMMERCIAL NAME	PURPOSE
Yellow F-G	For bright greenish yellows and greens.
Yellow F-3R	Workhorse color for most combination
(Golden yellow)	shades.
Scarlet F-3G	For bright red shades and for mixing black.
Red F-B	Workhorse color for most combination
(Fuchsia)	shades.
Blue F-R	Workhorse color for combination shades.
Navy F-2R	For rich browns and grays.

(There is no turquoise available with this series, reducing the range of mixed colors.)

terms to refer to one color (see Table 35). Without knowing the commercial name for the dye, the user has no way of telling which dye is being described. If the commercial names of the dyes being used are not specified in the catalog, request them.

TABLE 37

BASIC INVENTORY FOR PROCION H-E FIBER-REACTIVE DYES

COMMERCIAL NAME	PURPOSE
Yellow H-E6G	Workhorse dye for combination shades. Excellent compatibility with Turquoise H-A for producing bright greens.
Red H-E3B	Workhorse dye for combination shades.
Blue H-ERD	Useful for many combination shades.
Green H-E4BDA	Useful in place of turquoise for many com-
(Green-blue)	bination shades such as olive drab and forest green.
Navy H-ER	Dulling element for many dark, dull shades.
Turquoise H-A*	Especially useful for production of intense greens.

*An H series, not an H-E series dye. Excellent compatibility with most H-E dyes, and applied using the same dyeing procedure.

With the MX dyes, many similar hues are often produced to meet the demands of special industrial usage situations. For example, one particular red dye may have higher lightfastness than another. Table 35 shows a portion of the range of MX red dyes produced by Procion with the color descriptions used by some retailers.

Each distributor selects those dyes that he or she feels will best meet the needs of the customer. Since more than one dye may be suitable as a primary for color mixing purposes, one distributor may carry a different selection of dyes than another. This makes it difficult to recommend a basic inventory of MX dyes without limiting the dyer to purchasing from a selected few retailers. Instead, it is suggested that the user work with the dyes recommended by the retailer of his or her choice. Just remember that the dyes selected to serve as primaries must be consistently used. Otherwise, color mixing results will vary.

With the Cibacron F and the Procion H-E series fiber-reactive dyes a unique situation exists: currently, there is only one retailer for each series that offers these dyes to the home user in small quantities. (It is possible to purchase these dyes in one-pound or larger amounts from other sources.) The following lists give those dyes suggested by the retailer to be used as primaries for color mixing purposes.

A computer matching color service is available to the home dyer with the H-E series dyes. The service is made available by the retailer who handles the H-E dyes. The user submits a sample of the fiber and the color it is to be dyed, which are then analyzed by the computer. Results are expressed in terms of the percentages of the dyes needed to mix the color.

11. Evaluating and Exploring

Recording Dyeing Results

Because colors appear several shades darker when wet, allow fibers to dry thoroughly before evaluating dyeing results. Even if the color results do not appear as planned, record the dyeing information for future reference. All results are valuable, even if only to inform the dyer that a certain combination of colors

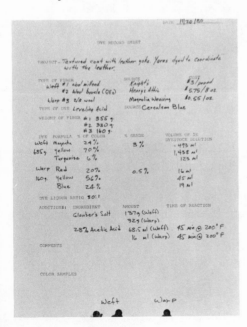

Example of a dye record sheet used for a particular weaving project.

A dye record sheet for color samples and dye formulas.

produces an undesirable shade. At some future time that particular color may be acceptable.

It is important for every dyer to keep good records so that dyeing results can be duplicated. A sample of the dyed yarn or fabric attached to the dye record sheet will provide a visual record for color matching purposes. Have a number of dye record sheets made up in advance to encourage yourself to write down dyeing information in a permanent form. It is quite easy to get into the habit of jotting down dye notes on a piece of scrap paper with good intentions of recopying at a later time. Unfortunately, however, scrap paper has a habit of ending up in the wastebasket before the information has been permanently recorded. A dyer's records are valuable property and should be treated with the same importance as the actual dyeing procedure.

For various reasons, not every dyeing procedure is successful. All dyers have a certain proportion of "cobblers"—a word used in industry to describe dyeings that do not pass inspection. Most unacceptable dye results occur for two reasons: the dyeing is uneven or the color does not appear as planned. Fortunately, there are certain steps with both the leveling acid and the fiber-reactive dyes that can be taken to correct both faults.

Causes of Uneven Dyeing

Streaky dyeing can be a result of:

(1) Dirty yarn. All yarns and fabrics must be thoroughly scoured prior to dyeing.

(2) Fiber not completely wetted before dyeing. Soak fiber a minimum of twenty minutes so that it can absorb dye solution at a uniform rate.

(3) Too rapid a temperature increase. The dye-fiber reaction should proceed slowly. If the temperature increases rapidly to boiling, the dye will react too quickly.

(4) Fiber not stirred during the exhaust and fixation phases. Gentle movement of the fiber insures even penetration of the dye.

(5) Failing to mix after adding the acid or alkali. The dye begins to react as soon as the acid or alkali is added. It must be evenly distributed throughout the dyebath before the fiber is replaced in the dyepot.

Correcting Streaky Dyeing with the Leveling Acid Dyes

Glauber's salt can be used quite successfully to correct streaky dyeing with the leveling acid dyes. (It does not have the same effect with the other acid dye classes.) Because the salt reduces

The unevenly dyed skein of wool on the left was evened up by simmering the yarn for thirty minutes in a waterbath with Glauber's salt to which acetic acid was then added to refix the dye. The skein on the right is the result of this treatment.

the attraction between the dye molecule and the wool fiber, the dye is able to become more evenly distributed throughout the fiber. Twenty percent Glauber's salt based on the weight of the fiber (fiber weight × 0.20) in a fresh-water bath should even out most dyeing results if allowed to simmer for thirty to sixty minutes. This process, however, will also remove some of the color, making it necessary to add additional acid (the same amount that was used for dyeing) to return the fiber to its original depth of color. (Other classes of dyes are more difficult to even up and require the use of commercial strippers. Information on how to use these should be available from the retailer who handles the dyes.)

If after the Glauber's salt treatment the fiber is still streaked, a weak alkali such as ammonia can be used to strip the dye from the fiber. Heat the fiber for thirty minutes at a temperature just below the boil with one-half percent ammonia based on the weight of the fiber (fiber weight × 0.005). Following this treatment, add acetic acid (the same amount used in the dye recipe) to return the dye to the fiber in a level manner. The stripping process with ammonia causes some damage to the fiber, however, and should be avoided unless absolutely necessary. An alternative solution is to hide the streaky results by dyeing the fiber a darker color.

Salvaging Uneven Dye Results with the Fiber-Reactive Dyes

A reducing agent such as Spectralite (see Suppliers) can be used to remove the majority of color from cellulose fibers which

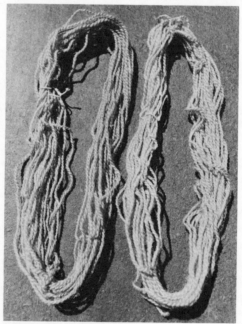

Lightening effect produced by simmering wool for thirty minutes in a waterbath with Glauber's salt. The skein on the right is the result of this treatment.

have been dyed with the fiber-reactive dyes. While it is not always possible to remove all of the color, enough will be stripped so that the fiber can be overdyed. According to one distributor, the chemical can even be used on clothes. Directions for use are available from distributors.

Altering Undesirable Color Results

The Glauber's salt treatment described above for the leveling acid dyes can also be used to change an unsatisfactory color, especially when the shade is too dark. If additional acid is not added, the stripped color is prevented from returning to the fiber. This results in an approximately 25 percent loss of color.

Dilute acetic acid can be used to lighten a dark color dyed with the fiber-reactive dyes. Add 1.5 to 3 mls of 28 percent acetic acid to

A dyer can achieve subtle variations in hue, value and intensity in a single dyebath by coloring various textures and natural-colored fibers together.

a liter of water, raise the temperature to between 160°F and 212°F and continue heating until the shade is reduced.

Other alternatives for changing a color include overdyeing an unsatisfactory color a darker shade, such as navy blue or brown. Overdyeing can also be used to alter the original color (see Chapter 5, Color, for a review of color mixing results). Orange, for example, may be overdyed with blue to obtain a duller shade or it can be overdyed with red to produce a different hue. Always proceed from a lighter color to a darker shade. If attempts to match a color are unsatisfactory, a readjustment of the dye for-

Tie-dyeing can be used to create many interesting color effects.

mula with additional experimenting is necessary. By using the above recommendations as a guide, just about any unsatisfactory dyeing with the leveling acid and the fiber-reactive dyes can be salvaged.

Creative Dyeing

Once a basic inventory of dye formulas has been obtained, the dyer can explore the potentials of color mixing. By using the available color samples as a reference standard, he or she can mix almost any color desired by varying the known formulas.

In addition, color variations can be achieved within a single dyepot by using different textured yarns and fibers as well as various natural-colored fibers such as gray, beige and cream. In this way, a subtle range of colors can be achieved from a single dye process. For example, a shiny nylon yarn, a fuzzy mohair, a natural gray wool and a two-ply white yarn in a dyebath of burnt orange will all yield different shades. Or, a natural cotton bouclé, a skein of cottolin (cotton-linen blend) and a mercerized cotton crochet yarn in the same dyebath would produce an exciting range of similar hues.

Other possibilities for creative dyeing include tie-dyeing, over-dyeing of commercially-dyed yarns and intentionally-produced unevenly-dyed yarns. Many books are available on tie-dyeing. To produce streaky yarns, try breaking some of the rules given for even dyeing. For example, purposely omit the Glauber's salt with the leveling acid dyes and do not stir the dyebath during the procedure. Or try throwing unwetted yarn into the dyepot. Exciting, individualized results can be obtained by knowledgeably manipulating the rules for even dyeing.

The fiber artist who is also a dyer enjoys benefits unknown to those who must purchase their yarns already dyed. Whether dyeing for practical or for artistic reasons, the person who has mastered the art of dyeing is in complete control. Like the painter, the dyer has an unlimited color palette ready for the mixing.

With the possibility of creating any color imagined, the dyer finds a new excitement in working with fiber. Now the only limitation is the imagination. The range of colors that can be mixed is waiting to be explored.

Appendix: Lanaset Dyes

In mid 1985, a combination wool-reactive and 1:2 premetallized dye series became available to the home dyer. These dyes, produced by Ciba-Geigy under the trade name of Lanaset, usually are marketed to the home dyer under the distributor's trade name.

Like the premetallized dyes, these dyes have very good fastness properties. In addition, they are available in a much brighter color range than the premetallized dyes, making it possible to mix both intense and subdued colors. And, because all of the dyes in the series have very similar dyeing properties, they can be used together in any desired combination. For the fiber artist whose work demands the use of a dye which provides both high wash and light fastness across the entire color spectrum, these dyes are an invaluable addition.

The Lanaset dyes are applied at a pH of 4.5-5, which is the most favorable pH for dyeing wool (known as the isoelectric point of wool), as fiber damage is minimized. Industry, for example, has recognized up to a 20% increase in fiber recovery following the processing of wool dyed with these dyes.

Other advantages of these dyes include almost total dye exhaustion with good reproducibility of colors. In addition, they are excellent dyes to use on silk and silk/wool blends, giving the same fastness properties as obtained with the premetallized dyes. And they also can be used with nylon.

The Lanaset dye series includes both bright and dull colors. Intense colors currently available to the home dyer include the Yellow 4G, Red 2B, Blue 2R (red blue), Blue 5G (blue green) and Violet B. There is no bright blue red (magenta) available in this series, although it is possible to use a magenta from the weak acid dyes (milling dyes) in combination with the dyes in this series.

The less intense colors in the series presently available to the home dyer include Yellow 2R, a gold yellow useful for mixing oranges as well as the deeper shades, Red G, a dull red useful for mixing browns and tans, Bordeaux BA, Navy R and Black. These shades are especially useful for mixing the heavier dull colors.

Chemicals Used with the Dyes

Albegal SET, developed by Ciba-Geigy for use with the Lanaset dyes, is a three-product mix that aids in leveling. This product often is sold to the home dyer under the distributor's trade name.

Albegal SET is used to improve the compatibility of the dye colors and promote their even exhaustion by slowing down the rate at which they move onto the fiber. In addition, the product enhances dye migra-

TABLE 38

FASTNESS PROPERTIES OF THE DYES

COLOR	LIGHT-FASTNESS	WASH-FASTNESS	COMMENTS
yellow (Yellow 4G)	5-6	4-5	clear, bright color
gold yellow (Yellow 2R)	6-7	5	useful for mixing deep shades and orange
red (Red 2B)	5-6	4-5	clear, bright color
red (Red G)	5-6	4-5	dull color useful for mixing browns
magenta (Bordeaux BA)	6-7	4-5	dull color
royal blue (Blue 2R)	5-6	4-5	clear, bright color
turquoise (Blue 5G)	5-6	4-5	clear, bright color
violet (Violet B)	4-5	5	very intense color
navy blue (Navy R)	5-6	5	useful for mixing deep, dull shades
black (Black B)	6-7	4-5	very strong color

tion. And it also helps the dye to penetrate the fiber. Without it, more dye would remain on the fiber surface where it could eventually be rubbed off and affect the washfastness of the dyeing.

Because Albegal SET is viscous, it is easier to measure in a diluted form (10% stock solution, for example) when dyeing small amounts of fiber. To prepare a 10% stock, add 10 ml Albegal SET for each 90 ml warm water.

The Glauber's salt, used in conjunction with the Albegal SET, also serves as a leveling agent at dyeings of pH 5 or below. At a higher pH, however, the salt may have the opposite effect and should be omitted (for example, when dyeing nylon).

The Depth of Shade of the dyeing determines how much Glauber's salt is used. Pale colors require the highest concentration (10% of fiber weight) because they are the most difficult to level. As the Depth of Shade increases, the concentration of salt decreases until, with deep values, no salt is needed.

Acetic acid is used to adjust the pH of the dyebath between 4.5-5, which is the range where fiber damage is minimized and maximum dye exhaustion occurs. This range gives up to 97% exhaustion with pale to medium colors.

The amount of acetic acid (1%-4%) needed to adjust the pH of the bath is dependent on the pH of the water source; the more acidic the water, the less acid needed to obtain the proper pH. The first time the dyes are used, the percent of acetic acid is determined experimentally. Thereafter, the percent of acetic acid should remain constant as long as the pH of the water source does not change.

After adding the chemicals to the dyebath, determine its pH by placing a small drop of the solution on pH paper. Match the color that appears with the corresponding color on the chart that comes with the paper. Each color denotes a specific pH. Select a pH paper that gives readings in the acid range (less than pH 7).

Often the pH of the dyebath fluctuates during the dyeing and does not remain within the optimum range (pH 4.5-5). To see if this has occurred, check the dyebath pH when dyeing is completed. If the final pH is above 5, add sodium acetate to all future dyeings. The combination of sodium acetate and acetic acid creates a buffered solution that helps maintain the proper pH range.

Notes on the Dyeing Procedure

The first ten-minute soak with the auxiliary chemicals (Albegal SET, Glauber's salt and acetic acid), followed by a second ten-minute soak after the dye has been added, allow the fiber to become thoroughly saturated with these chemicals and the dye to be evenly distributed. Both of the ten-minute soaks take place at 120° F., a temperature at which neither exhaustion nor chemical fixation occurs. As the temperature of the dyebath is raised, however, the dye begins exhausting onto the fiber where it then is chemically bound. For this reason, it is important to raise the temperature slowly (45-50 minutes) and stir frequently so that the dye can be applied evenly. Exhaustion occurs at a steady rate up to 170° F., then accelerates slightly up to boil. If leveling is a problem, hold the temperature at 170° F. for 15-20 minutes to give the dye additional time to even.

Once the dyebath is at temperature (190°-212° F.), hold it at this point for 15-40 minutes to give the dye time to complete exhaustion and fixation. The length of this period depends on the final dyebath temperature; the higher the temperature, the faster the rate of exhaustion. Also, the elevated temperature, along with the Albegal SET, enhances fiber penetration by the dye and minimizes the chance of surface dyeing.

Usually the dyer is interested in obtaining an even, or level, dyeing. A slow temperature rise coupled with frequent stirring are the two most important factors in achieving this. Other conditions that affect leveling include too acid a dyebath (below pH 4.5), which causes a more rapid dye strike, and failure to achieve and hold a high enough temperature. Leveling continues to occur at the boil with these dyes.

TABLE 39

LANASET DYEING PROCEDURE

Ingredients	Volume of Hot water (120°F)	+	Weight of Glauber's salt (g)	+	Volume of 10% Albegal SET stock (ml)	+	Volume of 56% Acetic Acid (ml)	+	Weight of Sodium Acetate (g)
Amount	fiber weight (g) × dye liquor ratio (usually 20 ml water per 1 g fiber)		fiber weight × percent of Glauber's salt*		fiber weight × 10% (if working with undiluted Albegal SET use fiber weight × 1%)		fiber weight × 1%–4% (add volume that will give pH 4.5-5. Check with pH paper.)		fiber weight × 2%–4% (use only if pH of dye bath has risen above pH 5 at end of dyeing procedure; check with pH paper).

Procedure: Add hot water, Glauber's salt, Albegal SET and acetic acid to dye pot and mix well. Check with pH paper; if bath is above pH 5, add more acetic acid. Enter previously scoured and wetted fiber to dye pot and stir. Hold for 10 minutes at 120° F.

ADD

Ingredient	Volume of 1% dyestock solutions (ml)
Amount	fiber weight × DOS × % of color (mix dye colors in separate containers or remove fiber before adding dye to pot)

Procedure: Add dye and mix well. Replace fiber if previously removed and hold at 120° F for 10 minutes; stir occasionally. Slowly raise the temperature of the dyebath to a boil over a period of 45-50 minutes. Stir frequently. Hold at boiling for 15-40 minutes until dyebath exhausts (at pale to medium DOS up to 97% exhaustion is possible). When dyeing silk, do not raise temperature above 190° F.

Finishing: At completion of dyeing procedure, check pH. If the pH has risen above 5, add sodium acetate to all future dyeings. Allow dyebath to cool, then wash fiber with a mild detergent and rinse well.

*The amount of Glauber's salt depends on the DOS as follows:

Depth of Shade	% of Glauber's salt
less than 0.5%	10%
0.5%–less than 1%	5%
1%–2%	2.5%
greater than 2%	0%

Up to 97% dye exhaustion is possible with the Lanaset dyes. Factors that affect dye yield include too high a pH (above 5), which retards dye exhaustion, and failure to run at a high enough temperature. Also too high a concentration of either the Albegal SET or the Glauber's salt will reduce the dye yield.

Dyeing Silk

The dyeing procedure for silk is the same as for wool except that the final dyebath temperature should not exceed 190° F. to minimize fiber damage. Also, silk does not require as high a temperature for dye penetration to occur. Silk dyed in combination with wool will appear slightly different than silk dyed alone: experiment to determine the difference.

Dyeing Nylon

Nylon is more difficult to dye evenly than the protein fibers because a strong affinity exists between the fiber and the dye. Acetic acid, which is normally used to encourage dye exhaustion and to establish a favorable pH range to minimize fiber damage, should not be used as it causes the dye to react too rapidly. Also, nylon does not require the fiber protection provided by a pH of 4.5-5. Instead, nylon should be dyed at a pH of 6.5-8. In addition, omit the Glauber's salt since it does not function as a leveling agent above pH 5. The Albegal SET, however, should be added to the dyebath.

Preparation of Stock Solution

A convenient method for preparing Lanaset stock solutions is to first paste the dye powder with hot water (120° F.). Then bring the pasted dye up to volume with very hot (170° F.) water. Avoid using boiling water when preparing Lanaset stock solutions, as it may cause the dye molecules to clump.

If the dye has been pasted in a small container such as a plastic cup, transfer the paste to a larger vessel by thoroughly rinsing the container with small volumes of hot water. A wash bottle (see Supply Sources) is an effective tool to use for rinsing. Store stock solutions in a properly labeled container with a tight-fitting lid and keep in a cool, dark area where children do not have access.

No matter how carefully the stock solution is prepared, the gold yellow dye (Yellow 2R) will rapidly settle out. To obtain reproducible results, swirl the stock solution each time before measuring. It is a good idea to always check all stock solutions before measuring to be certain there is no sediment. If settling has occurred, redissolve the dye by heating in a pan of hot water.

Glossary

Acid Dye. A dye that is a salt of an organic acid and requires an acid or an acid-producing compound in the dyebath as a dyeing assistant. Acid dyes have a chemical affinity for protein fibers.

Additive Color Mixing. A result of the mixing or blending of colored lights. Additive color mixtures create additional light energy so that a lighter color is produced. The additive primaries are red, green and blue. A blend of the additive primaries in equal amounts produces white.

Adsorption. Assimilation of the dye on the fiber surface only (*not* throughout the fiber).

All-Purpose, Union or Household Dye. A dye composed both of leveling acid dyes (for protein fibers) and direct dyes (for cellulose fibers). The result of this combination is that when one fiber type is dyed, the part of the dye specific for the other fiber type cannot react and is wasted, making such a dye expensive to use. These dyes are useful, however, for coloring protein-cellulose fiber blends.

Amino Acid. An organic compound containing both an amino group (NH_2) and a carboxylic acid group (COOH). Amino acids are the building blocks of protein.

Amorphous Areas. Portions of the fiber where the polymer chains are randomly arranged. These areas are easily dyed.

Auxochrome. The portion of the dye molecule that influences the intensity of the dye. It also provides the site where the chemical bonding with the fiber occurs.

Cellulose Fiber. Any fiber produced by a plant: for example, cotton, linen, jute and ramie. Cellulose, like sugar and starch, is a carbohydrate composed of carbon, hydrogen and oxygen. Of importance to the dyer is the presence in all cellulose fibers of the chemically reactive hydroxyl (^-OH) groups, which can react with the dye molecule.

Chromophore. The color-producing part of the dye molecule.

Classes of Dyes. A classification of dye types based on how they are used.

Cold Type Fiber-reactive Dye. A dye so highly reactive that the chemical bonding can take place at room temperature. Examples are Procion MX and Cibacron F.

Colour Index (or C.I.) Name. The generic name used for a particular dye. (See preceding.)

Complementary Color. The color directly opposite another on the color wheel.

Continuous Dyeing. A dyeing procedure in which the dye is directly applied to the fiber, as in textile printing. Continuous dyeing methods do not require an affinity of the dye for the fiber.

Crystalline Areas. The portions of a fiber where the polymer chains are arranged in parallel order. It is difficult for the dye to penetrate these areas.

Depth of Shade. The value of a color as determined by the volume of dyestock solution used to dye a certain weight of fiber.

Diffusion. The movement of the dye molecules in the waterbath. Diffusion is influenced by the temperature of the dyebath and the type of fiber being dyed.

Direct Dye. A cellulose-fiber dye possessing only good to fair washfastness because of weak chemical bonds between the dye and the fiber. The dye, which is easy to apply, requires salt to promote exhaustion.

Dye Liquor. The water used in the dyebath.

Dye Liquor Ratio. The proportion of water (by weight) to a given weight of fiber. In the metric system, there is equivalence between the weight and volume of water (one milliliter of water weighs one gram), allowing the water to be measured as a volume.

Dyeing Assistants. Chemicals used to alter the conditions of a dye reaction: for example, an acid used to lower the pH of the dyebath.

Dyestock Solution. A concentrated solution of dye dissolved in water. The amount of dye powder in the water is expressed as a percentage: for example, a 1% dyestock solution means there is one gram of dye powder for each 100 mls of water.

Electrolytes. Substances that chemically come apart in solution (usually water), forming positively and negatively charged ions. All salts are electrolytes, and chemical salts are an important class of compounds used in dyeing.

Exhaust. The movement of the dye from the water onto the fiber.

Exhaust Dyeing. A dyeing procedure in which the fiber is immersed in a water bath in which the dye has been dissolved. An affinity of the dye for the fiber is necessary with this dyeing method.

Exhaust Phase. The first stage of the dye reaction, when the dye moves from the water onto the fiber. Leveling has a chance to occur during this phase.

Fast Acid (or supermilling) Dye. A type of acid dye applied from a neutral or just slightly acid solution. The high molecular weight of the fast acid dyes gives them good washfastness but makes leveling difficult. Dye colors are bright.

Fastness. The ability of a dye to resist fading following application.

Fiber-Reactive Dye. A synthetic dye, used with the cellulose fibers, requiring the use of salt and an alkali as dyeing assistants. The name "fiber-reactive" refers to the type of chemical bonding that occurs; the dye chemically becomes a part of the fiber.

Fixation Phase. The second stage of the dyeing procedure, when the dye reacts or bonds chemically with the fiber.

Gradation. The gradual movement from one color to another. The color progression can be from one hue to another, one value to the next, or one shade or tone to another, with the number of steps in the gradation determined by the degree of color movement desired.

Graduated Cylinder. A calibrated container used to measure amounts larger than can be accommodated by a pipette.

Gram. A metric unit of weight. There are 454 grams to a pound and 28 grams to an ounce.

Hot Type Fiber-Reactive Dye. A dye that requires heat for the fixation to occur. Examples are Procion H and H-E dyes.

Hue. A specific color such as red, green or blue.

Hydrolysis. The reaction of a chemical compound with a hydroxyl ($^-$OH) group in water.

Ikat. A method of dyeing where the warp and/or weft is tie-dyed to create unusual design and color effects. When the yarns are woven, a slight blurring effect occurs because of the shifting of the yarns during the warping and/or weaving procedure.

Intensity. The brightness of a color.

Intermediate Color. The color produced by combining a primary and an adjacent secondary color in less than equal amounts.

Ion. An atom, group of atoms or a molecule that has acquired either a positive or a negative electrical charge as a result of gaining or losing electrons.

Ionic Bond. A chemical bond created by electron sharing between two or more atoms of opposite electrical charge. For example, with the acid dyes, an ionic bond is formed between the positively charged amino acids on the protein molecule and the negatively charged portion of the dye molecule.

Kiton Dye. *(See Leveling Acid Dye.)*

Leveling. The process where a dye becomes evenly distributed on the fiber surface. A dye that levels well produces even dye results.

Leveling Acid Dye. A type of acid dye, used with the protein fibers, that requires a strong acid as a dyeing assistant. The name "leveling acid" refers to the ability of the dye to achieve even or level dyeings.

Leveling Agent. A chemical that promotes the even distribution of the dye on the fiber surface. Glauber's salt is an example of a leveling agent used with the leveling acid dyes.

Liter. The metric unit of volume. A liter is slightly larger than a quart.

Meniscus. The concave surface formed where a liquid touches the glass wall of a pipette or graduated cylinder. All readings are made at the bottom of the meniscus.

Meter. The metric unit of length.

Milliliter. One thousandth of a liter. Five milliliters are equivalent to one teaspoon.

Monomer. An individual molecular unit. Monomers are capable of joining together to form long chains.

1:2 Prematallized Dye. An acid dye to which a metal atom is attached for the purpose of improving washfastness. "1:2" indicates there is a ratio of one metal atom for each two dye molecules.

Overdyeing. A dyeing technique used to alter a color by redyeing it a new shade. The overdyed shade is always darker than the original color.

Percent of Color. The percentage of each dyestock solution that makes up a mixed color.

Pipette. A metrically calibrated glass tube, similar to a straw, with a point on one end. A pipette is used to measure small volumes of liquid.

Polymer. A long molecular chain composed of many similar molecular units or monomers joined together in an orderly manner.

Polypeptide Chain. A long molecular chain composed of certain amino acids that are linked together. Each protein fiber is made up of polypeptide chains of specific composition and arrangement.

Primary Color. A color that cannot itself be mixed from a combination of other colors but which, when mixed with the other primary colors, produces almost all the other colors. The primary colors of the dyer are the subtractive primaries magenta, turquoise and yellow, with red and blue added to extend the color mixing range.

Protein Fiber. A fiber produced by an animal or an insect. All protein fibers are composed of amino acids, with each fiber having a specific number and type of acids. Wool, silk, alpaca and cashmere are examples of protein fibers.

Reducing Agent. Any chemical that removes oxygen. A reducing agent is used with the vat dyes.

Secondary Color. The color produced when two primary colors are combined in equal amounts. Violet, green and orange are the secondary colors.

Shade. A hue plus black. In dyeing, a color can also be darkened by adding its complement.

Stock Solution Method of Dyeing. The dyeing procedure in which the dye is measured as a solution rather than as a powder. This allows for the accurate measurement of the dye with inexpensive volumetric equipment. Expensive scales, on the other hand, are needed to measure the dye as a powder.

Substantivity. The affinity of a dye (as opposed to the affinity of water) for the fiber in the dyebath. The higher the substantivity of the dye for the fiber, the more dye adsorbed by the fiber. This characteristic of a dye is especially important with the fiber-reactive dyes because they are also capable of reacting chemically with the water.

Subtractive Color Mixing. A result of the mixing or blending of dyes and pigments. A loss of light energy occurs each time subtractive colors are mixed, so the resulting color is always darker than its parent colors. The subtractive primaries are magenta, cyan (turquoise) and yellow.

Supermilling Dye. *(See Fast Acid Dye.)*

Tertiary Color. A color composed of any proportion of all three colors, all three primary colors, or a primary and the secondary opposite it on the color wheel. The resultant colors are less intense than their parent colors because of the darkening effect produced by subtractive color mixing.

Tie-Dyeing. A method of dyeing in which the fabric, yarn or fiber is tightly tied in certain areas to prevent dye penetration.

Tint. A hue plus white. In dyeing, a tint is created by using less dye in the dyepot.

Tone. A hue plus gray. In dyeing, a tone can also be achieved by adding some of a color's complement to the tint of the color.

Trichromatic Blend. A color mixing scheme where the three primary dyes are blended in a systematic fashion to produce intermediate, secondary and tertiary colors.

Unfixed Dye. The dye that has not chemically reacted with the fiber. With the fiber-reactive dyes, the unfixed dye is readily hydrolyzed (it reacts with water) and cannot be reused. Any acid dye that has not reacted with the fiber, however, can be used to color additional fiber.

Vat Dye. A type of dye not soluble in water in its natural state but which, when treated with a reducing agent, is converted into a water-soluble form that can then be applied to fiber. Once inside the fiber the dye is changed back into its insoluble form by oxidation, and trapped. Vat dyes generally possess very good washfastness and lightfastness.

Supply Sources

The following sources are included as an aid in locating equipment and supplies for exhaust dyeing. I have detailed the equipment and supplies that each dealer carried at the time of publication and are relevant to the material presented in the book. (The list is not intended, of course, to suggest that this is all a dealer stocks.) For up-to-date information, it's a good idea to contact a supplier and request a catalog, for which there is a charge in some cases.

There are many dye-supply sources besides those listed here, including local art and craft stores. (Where I live, for example, two weaving shops carry a complete inventory of dye supplies.) Fiber-related magazines are another good source for locating suppliers. However, the dyer should be aware that some dealers are geared specifically toward those fiber artists doing surface-design work such as batik, and dyeing instructions from those dealers will be designed for that particular type of work.

Refer to Chapter 10, "Where to Begin", for information on which dyes to order. When requesting information from a dealer, always include a large self-addressed stamped envelope to ensure an immediate response.

DYE SUPPLIERS *(many weaving shops also carry dyes; check there first)*

Cerulean Blue P.O. Box 21168 Seattle, WA 98111-3168 (206) 443-7744	Lanaset dyes; leveling acid dyes; Deka dyes; Ciba Vat dyes; Cibacron F dyes. Catalog $3.25 (very informative)
Pro Chemical & Dye, Inc. P.O. Box 14 Somerset, MA 02726 (617) 676-3838	Lanaset dyes; leveling acid dyes; Procion M dyes; Cibacron F dyes; Procion H dyes; Washfast acid dyes (weak acid and super milling dyes). Free price list.
Keystone-Ingham Corp. P.O. Box 1296 La Mirada, CA 90637 (213) 802-3937	Leveling acid dyes; Procion M dyes; premetallized dyes; Lanaset dyes; Cibacron F dyes. Free price list; $50 minimum order

SCIENTIFIC EQUIPMENT SUPPLIERS

Cerulean Blue P.O. Box 21168 Seattle, WA 98111-3168 (206) 443-7744	Safety equipment, scale, wash bottle, pH paper, beakers, pipette (10 ml), pipette bulb, thermometer. Catalog $3.25 (very informative).
Pro Chemical & Dye, Inc. P.O. Box 14 Somerset, MA 02726 (617) 676-3838	Scale, triple-beam balance, thermometer, safety equipment, beakers, pipettes (1 ml, 5 ml, 10 ml, 25 ml), graduated cylinders.
Scientific Supply and Equipment 1818 East Madison St. Seattle, WA 98122 (206) 324-8550 1-800-552-7164 (WA only) 1-800-426-0455 (OR, ID, MT & Northern CA)	Dye industry pipettes: 10 ml pipette, catalog #13-671 109M; 1 ml pipette, catalog #13-671 109F. All scientific equipment mentioned in book. $5 handling charge for orders less than $25. All orders prepaid.

SCIENTIFIC EQUIPMENT SUPPLIERS (continued)

Allied Fisher Scientific P.O. Box 1148 Kent, WA 98032 (206) 872-0330 (or check Yellow Pages for closest branch office)	Dye industry pipettes: same catalog numbers as listed above. Also all scientific equipment mentioned in book. $50 minimum order, prepaid.
All-World Scientific and Chemical 3259 20th Avenue West Seattle, WA 98199 (206) 282-2133 1-800-562-2855 (WA only)	All scientific equipment mentioned in book except pipettes.

SUPPLIERS OF CHEMICALS USED FOR DYEING

Cerulean Blue P.O. Box 21168 Seattle, WA 98111-3168 (206) 443-7744	Glauber's salt, 56% acetic acid, washing soda, Synthrapol, Calgon, Thiourea Dioxide, Albegal SET, hand cleaning paste
Pro Chemical & Dye, Inc. P.O. Box 14 Somerset, MA 02726 (617) 676-3838	Glauber's salt, 56% acetic acid, washing soda, Calgon, Synthrapol, hand cleaner, Albegal SET
Keystone-Ingham P.O. Box 1296 La Mirada, CA 90637 (213) 802-3937	Glauber's salt, Albegal SET.

MISCELLANEOUS

Shades of Wool 15280 Douglas Rd. Yakima, WA 98908	Color sample book for leveling acid dye. 373 color samples in two values. Color sample book for Lanaset dyes. Send SASE for information.
Color Trends Michan Enterprises 8037 9th NW Seattle, WA 98117	Bi-yearly magazine containing fiber facts, dye information and fashion color forecast. Dyed fiber samples included. $32 per year (two issues).

Index

Acetic acid: use of, with leveling acid dyes, 29, 36, 114; use of, with basic dyes, 44; concentrated, how to dilute, 114; measurement of, 114; sources of, 114; importance of removing after dyeing, 114; use of, for color lightening, 147

Acid dyes: defined, 28-29, 34; classes of, 34; dyestock solution, life of, 104; dyestock solution, preparation of, 106-107; See also Leveling acid dyes, Premetallized dyes, Supermilling dyes

Additive color mixing: defined, 69; primary colors of, 69 (photograph); effect of, on light energy, 70

All-purpose dyes; 44, 62 (table)

Ammonia: use of, for correcting uneven dyeings, 146

Ammonium sulfate: use of, with acid dyes, 39-40, 42

Amorphous areas of fiber, 22 (diagram), 23

Anderson, Ruth E.: work of, 9 (photograph)

Auxochrome, 18

Azoic dyes, 46, 60, 62 (table)

Basic dyes, 43 (table), 44

Benefits of dyeing: controlling color, 3, 5-9, 6-9 (photographs), 123, 149; saving money, 3-5, 7 (photograph)

Black: location on color wheel, 78, 80

Brown: location on color wheel, 77, 80; analysis of parentage, 78

Brown, Peter G.: work of, C3

Bryant, Laura Militzer: work of, C2

Calgon: 118

Cellulose fibers: factors to consider when selecting a dye for, 20-21; examples of, 22, 31 (diagram), 45; chemistry of, 30; how dye reaction affected by structure of, 31; dye classes used with, 44 (table), 62

Chrome mordant dyes, 40, 43 (table)

Chromophore: defined, 18; effect of, on lightfastness of leveling acid dyes, 19-20, 38; effect of, on lightfastness of fiber-reactive dyes, 56; general effects of, 67, 78

Cibacron F dyes: properties of, 16, 48, 49 (table); defined, 48; life of, in dyestock solution, 49, 104; uses of 49 (table), 50-51; dyeing procedure for 52-53, 122, 120 (table); ratings for fastness properties, 57 (table); in dyeing of silk, 122; purchasing of, 141 (table). See also Fiber-reactive dyes.

"Cold" type reactive dyes, 32, 47 (diagram)

Color; seeing of, 65-67; effect of light on, 68; measurement of, 67 (graph), 68; methods of mixing, 68-71; 69, 71 (diagrams)

"Color Compass", 80

Color gradation: defined, 123; importance of, 123-125; types of, 124-133

Color lightening: for leveling acid dyes, 146 (photograph), 147; for fiber-reactive dyes, 147

Color samples: importance of, 83, 124-125, 134-135, 148; method for producing, 125, 134-136; basic inventory of, 134-135; keeping records of, 143-144. See also Color gradations.

Color spectrum: how formed, 65 (diagram)

Color wheel: primary color systems for, 74-75, 75 (diagram), use of, in color mixing, 75-78, 81-82 (diagrams?), 82-83; and color orientation, 76 (diagram), 76-78; adapting for mixed dye colors, 78-79 (diagram)

Colour Index: described, 14; importance of, 14; examples of use of, 14

Colour Index Name: defined, 14; importance of, when purchasing acid dyes, 137-138

Colour Index Number: defined, 14

Complement. See Complementary color

Complementary color: defined, 64, 128, 129 (diagram); use of, for darkening colors, 64, 128-130.

Complement gradation: importance of, 128-130; defined, 129; color movement with, 129-130; example of, 131 (table)

Continuous dyeing, 32-33, 48

Converting ounces to grams, 87 (photograph)

Covalent bonding, 20, 25, 47; defined, 31; importance of, 31, 56. See also Fiber-reactive dyes

Crystalline areas of fiber: 22 (diagram), 23, 25-26

Daly, Lynn: work of, 7

Darwall, Randall: work of, C8

Depth of shade: defined (formula given), 108-109; calculation of (with example), 109; relationship of, to color value, 110 (table), 109

Diffusion: how affects removal of unfixed fiber-reactive dye, 56

Direct dyes, 46, 61, 62 (table)

Dye: ideal properties of, 9-10 (table);